Presented to

....

From

....

On this date

....

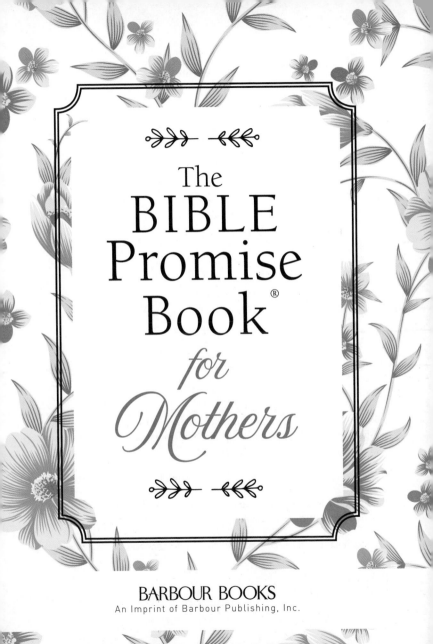

The
BIBLE
Promise
Book®

for
Mothers

BARBOUR BOOKS
An Imprint of Barbour Publishing, Inc.

© 2008 by Barbour Publishing, Inc.

ISBN 978-1-64352-310-1

All scripture quotations are taken from the King James Version of the Bible.

Published by Barbour Books, an imprint of Barbour Publishing, Inc., 1810 Barbour Drive, Uhrichsville, Ohio 44683, www.barbourbooks.com

Our mission is to inspire the world with the life-changing message of the Bible.

Member of the
Evangelical Christian
Publishers Association

Printed in China.

Introduction

Our world sends many conflicting signals on the important issues of life. How should we approach anger? Is discipline a good thing or not? Why speak with honesty? Is prayer for real? What is true wisdom?

In His kindness, God has answered all of these questions—and many more—in the pages of His Word, the Bible. Whatever our needs, we can find in scripture the principles we need to address the issues we face.

This collection of Bible verses is a handy reference to some of the key issues that all people—and especially mothers—face. In these pages, you'll find carefully selected verses that address topics like comfort, encouragement, friendship, purity, rest, and understanding. In fact, more than five dozen categories are covered, arranged alphabetically for ease of use.

This book is not intended to replace regular, personal Bible study. Nor is it a replacement for a good concordance for in-depth study of a particular subject. It is, however, a quick reference to some of the key issues of life that mothers most often face. We hope it will be an encouragement to you as you read.

Contents

Ability

And I give unto them eternal life; and they shall never perish, neither shall any man pluck them out of my hand. My Father, which gave them me, is greater than all; and no man is able to pluck them out of my Father's hand.

JOHN 10:28–29

But Jesus answered and said, Ye know not what ye ask. Are ye able to drink of the cup that I shall drink of, and to be baptized with the baptism that I am baptized with? They say unto him, We are able.

MATTHEW 20:22

For the which cause I also suffer these things: nevertheless I am not ashamed: for I know whom I have believed, and am persuaded that he is able to keep that which I have committed unto him against that day.

2 TIMOTHY 1:12

And being not weak in faith, he considered not his own body now dead, when he was about an hundred years old, neither yet the deadness of Sarah's womb: He staggered not at the promise of God through unbelief; but was strong in faith, giving glory to God; And being fully persuaded that, what he had promised, he was able also to perform.

Romans 4:19–21

Now unto him that is able to do exceeding abundantly above all that we ask or think, according to the power that worketh in us, unto him be glory in the church by Christ Jesus throughout all ages, world without end. Amen.

Ephesians 3:20–21

There hath no temptation taken you but such as is common to man: but God is faithful, who will not suffer you to be tempted above that ye are able; but will with the temptation also make a way to escape, that ye may be able to bear it.

1 CORINTHIANS 10:13

Jehoshaphat stood in the congregation of Judah and Jerusalem. . .And said, O LORD God of our fathers, art not thou God in heaven? and rulest not thou over all the kingdoms of the heathen? and in thine hand is there not power and might, so that none is able to withstand thee?

2 CHRONICLES 20:5–6

For in that he himself hath suffered being tempted, he is able to succour them that are tempted.

HEBREWS 2:18

And God is able to make all grace abound toward you; that ye, always having all sufficiency in all things, may abound to every good work.

2 CORINTHIANS 9:8

Now unto him that is able to keep you from falling, and to present you faultless before the presence of his glory with exceeding joy, To the only wise God our Saviour, be glory and majesty, dominion and power, both now and ever. Amen.

JUDE 24–25

Wherefore lay apart all filthiness and superfluity of naughtiness, and receive with meekness the engrafted word, which is able to save your souls.

JAMES 1:21

Adversity

For as the sufferings of Christ abound in us, so our consolation also aboundeth by Christ. And whether we be afflicted, it is for your consolation and salvation, which is effectual in the enduring of the same sufferings which we also suffer: or whether we be comforted, it is for your consolation and salvation.

2 CORINTHIANS 1:5–6

That the trial of your faith, being much more precious than of gold that perisheth, though it be tried with fire, might be found unto praise and honour and glory at the appearing of Jesus Christ.

1 PETER 1:7

If ye be reproached for the name of Christ, happy are ye; for the spirit of glory and of God resteth upon you: on their part he is evil spoken of, but on your part he is glorified.

1 PETER 4:14

For I reckon that the sufferings of this present time are not worthy to be compared with the glory which shall be revealed in us.

ROMANS 8:18

These things I have spoken unto you, that in me ye might have peace. In the world ye shall have tribulation: but be of good cheer; I have overcome the world.

JOHN 16:33

The righteous cry, and the LORD heareth, and delivereth them out of all their troubles.

PSALM 34:17

Yea, and all that will live godly in Christ Jesus shall suffer persecution.

2 TIMOTHY 3:12

Is any among you afflicted? let him pray.

JAMES 5:13

But the God of all grace, who hath called us unto his eternal glory by Christ Jesus, after that ye have suffered a while, make you perfect, stablish, strengthen, settle you.

1 PETER 5:10

Blessed are ye, when men shall hate you, and when they shall separate you from their company, and shall reproach you, and cast out your name as evil, for the Son of man's sake.

LUKE 6:22

Beloved, think it not strange concerning the fiery trial which is to try you, as though some strange thing happened unto you: But rejoice, inasmuch as ye are partakers of Christ's sufferings; that, when his glory shall be revealed, ye may be glad also with exceeding joy.

1 PETER 4:12–13

For this is thankworthy, if a man for conscience toward God endure grief, suffering wrongfully. . . . For even hereunto were ye called: because Christ also suffered for us, leaving us an example, that ye should follow his steps: Who did no sin, neither was guile found in his mouth: Who, when he was reviled, reviled not again; when he suffered, he threatened not; but committed himself to him that judgeth righteously.

1 PETER 2:19, 21–23

For our light affliction, which is but for a moment, worketh for us a far more exceeding and eternal weight of glory.

2 CORINTHIANS 4:17

If we suffer, we shall also reign with him.

2 TIMOTHY 2:12

Anger

He that is slow to wrath is of great understanding: but he that is hasty of spirit exalteth folly.

Proverbs 14:29

Wherefore, my beloved brethren, let every man be swift to hear, slow to speak, slow to wrath: For the wrath of man worketh not the righteousness of God.

James 1:19–20

Do all things without murmurings and disputings.

Philippians 2:14

Make no friendship with an angry man; and with a furious man thou shalt not go: Lest thou learn his ways, and get a snare to thy soul.

Proverbs 22:24–25

Be not hasty in thy spirit to be angry: for anger resteth in the bosom of fools.

Ecclesiastes 7:9

It is better to dwell in the wilderness, than with a contentious and an angry woman.

PROVERBS 21:19

Fathers, provoke not your children to anger, lest they be discouraged.

COLOSSIANS 3:21

But I say unto you, That whosoever is angry with his brother without a cause shall be in danger of the judgment: and whosoever shall say to his brother, Raca, shall be in danger of the council: but whosoever shall say, Thou fool, shall be in danger of hell fire.

MATTHEW 5:22

A wrathful man stirreth up strife: but he that is slow to anger appeaseth strife.

PROVERBS 15:18

He that is slow to anger is better than the mighty; and he that ruleth his spirit than he that taketh a city.

PROVERBS 16:32

Dearly beloved, avenge not yourselves, but rather give place unto wrath: for it is written, Vengeance is mine; I will repay, saith the Lord.

ROMANS 12:19

A soft answer turneth away wrath: but grievous words stir up anger.

PROVERBS 15:1

Better is a dry morsel, and quietness therewith, than an house full of sacrifices with strife.

PROVERBS 17:1

Be ye angry, and sin not: let not the sun go down upon your wrath.

EPHESIANS 4:26

Charity

Charge them that are rich in this world, that they be not highminded, nor trust in uncertain riches, but in the living God, who giveth us richly all things to enjoy; That they do good, that they be rich in good works, ready to distribute, willing to communicate; laying up in store for themselves a good foundation against the time to come, that they may lay hold on eternal life.

1 Timothy 6:17–19

Blessed is he that considereth the poor: the Lord will deliver him in time of trouble. The Lord will preserve him, and keep him alive; and he shall be blessed upon the earth: and thou wilt not deliver him unto the will of his enemies.

Psalm 41:1–2

I have been young, and now am old; yet have I not seen the righteous forsaken, nor his seed begging bread. He is ever merciful, and lendeth; and his seed is blessed.

PSALM 37:25–26

But when thou makest a feast, call the poor, the maimed, the lame, the blind: And thou shalt be blessed; for they cannot recompense thee: for thou shalt be recompensed at the resurrection of the just.

LUKE 14:13–14

Sell that ye have, and give alms; provide yourselves bags which wax not old, a treasure in the heavens that faileth not, where no thief approacheth, neither moth corrupteth. For where your treasure is, there will your heart be also.

LUKE 12:33–34

Give, and it shall be given unto you; good measure, pressed down, and shaken together, and running over, shall men give into your bosom. For with the same measure that ye mete withal it shall be measured to you again.

LUKE 6:38

He hath dispersed, he hath given to the poor; his righteousness endureth for ever.

PSALM 112:9

He that hath pity upon the poor lendeth unto the LORD; and that which he hath given will he pay him again.

PROVERBS 19:17

Comfort

⋙ ⋘

Blessed be God, even the Father of our Lord Jesus Christ, the Father of mercies, and the God of all comfort; Who comforteth us in all our tribulation, that we may be able to comfort them which are in any trouble, by the comfort wherewith we ourselves are comforted of God.

2 CORINTHIANS 1:3–4

Yea, though I walk through the valley of the shadow of death, I will fear no evil: for thou art with me; thy rod and thy staff they comfort me.

PSALM 23:4

For the LORD will not cast off for ever: But though he cause grief, yet will he have compassion according to the multitude of his mercies. For he doth not afflict willingly nor grieve the children of men.

LAMENTATIONS 3:31–33

And many of the Jews came to Martha and Mary, to comfort them concerning their brother.

JOHN 11:19

Nevertheless God, that comforteth those that are cast down, comforted us by the coming of Titus; And not by his coming only, but by the consolation wherewith he was comforted in you, when he told us your earnest desire, your mourning, your fervent mind toward me; so that I rejoiced the more.

2 CORINTHIANS 7:6–7

In the multitude of my thoughts within me thy comforts delight my soul.

PSALM 94:19

The LORD is my rock, and my fortress, and my deliverer; my God, my strength, in whom I will trust; my buckler, and the horn of my salvation, and my high tower.

PSALM 18:2

The LORD is good, a strong hold in the day of trouble; and he knoweth them that trust in him.

NAHUM 1:7

Thou shalt increase my greatness, and comfort me on every side.

PSALM 71:21

Confidence

Beloved, if our heart condemn us not, then have we confidence toward God. And whatsoever we ask, we receive of him, because we keep his commandments, and do those things that are pleasing in his sight.

1 JOHN 3:21–22

Being confident of this very thing, that he which hath begun a good work in you will perform it until the day of Jesus Christ.

PHILIPPIANS 1:6

According to the eternal purpose which he purposed in Christ Jesus our Lord: In whom we have boldness and access with confidence by the faith of him.

EPHESIANS 3:11–12

It is better to trust in the LORD than to put confidence in man. It is better to trust in the LORD than to put confidence in princes.

PSALM 118:8–9

But Christ as a son over his own house; whose house are we, if we hold fast the confidence and the rejoicing of the hope firm unto the end.

HEBREWS 3:6

Though an host should encamp against me, my heart shall not fear: though war should rise against me, in this will I be confident.

PSALM 27:3

And now, little children, abide in him; that, when he shall appear, we may have confidence, and not be ashamed before him at his coming.

1 JOHN 2:28

By terrible things in righteousness wilt thou answer us, O God of our salvation; who art the confidence of all the ends of the earth, and of them that are afar off upon the sea.

PSALM 65:5

And this is the confidence that we have in him, that, if we ask any thing according to his will, he heareth us: And if we know that he hear us, whatsoever we ask, we know that we have the petitions that we desired of him.

1 JOHN 5:14–15

For the LORD shall be thy confidence, and shall keep thy foot from being taken.

PROVERBS 3:26

Conversation

Even so the tongue is a little member, and boasteth great things. Behold, how great a matter a little fire kindleth!

JAMES 3:5

Let your speech be alway with grace, seasoned with salt, that ye may know how ye ought to answer every man.

COLOSSIANS 4:6

If any man offend not in word, the same is a perfect man, and able also to bridle the whole body.

JAMES 3:2

Let your conversation be without covetousness; and be content with such things as ye have.

HEBREWS 13:5

A talebearer revealeth secrets: but he that is of a faithful spirit concealeth the matter.

PROVERBS 11:13

A fool uttereth all his mind: but a wise man keepeth it in till afterwards.

PROVERBS 29:11

A soft answer turneth away wrath: but grievous words stir up anger.

PROVERBS 15:1

The heart of the righteous studieth to answer: but the mouth of the wicked poureth out evil things.

PROVERBS 15:28

In the multitude of words there wanteth not sin: but he that refraineth his lips is wise.

PROVERBS 10:19

But now ye also put off all these; anger, wrath, malice, blasphemy, filthy communication out of your mouth.

Colossians 3:8

Be not rash with thy mouth, and let not thine heart be hasty to utter any thing before God: for God is in heaven, and thou upon earth: therefore let thy words be few.

Ecclesiastes 5:2

Set a watch, O Lord, before my mouth; keep the door of my lips.

Psalm 141:3

There is that speaketh like the piercings of a sword: but the tongue of the wise is health.

Proverbs 12:18

A man hath joy by the answer of his mouth: and a word spoken in due season, how good is it!

PROVERBS 15:23

The heart of the wise teacheth his mouth, and addeth learning to his lips. Pleasant words are as an honeycomb, sweet to the soul, and health to the bones.

PROVERBS 16:23–24

For he that will love life, and see good days, let him refrain his tongue from evil, and his lips that they speak no guile.

1 PETER 3:10

A time to rend, and a time to sew; a time to keep silence, and a time to speak.

ECCLESIASTES 3:7

Courage

〰〰〰 〰〰〰

Only be thou strong and very courageous, that thou mayest observe to do according to all the law, which Moses my servant commanded thee: turn not from it to the right hand or to the left, that thou mayest prosper whithersoever thou goest.

JOSHUA 1:7

And now, little children, abide in him; that, when he shall appear, we may have confidence, and not be ashamed before him at his coming.

1 JOHN 2:28

Be ye therefore very courageous to keep and to do all that is written in the book of the law of Moses, that ye turn not aside therefrom to the right hand or to the left.

JOSHUA 23:6

Wait on the LORD: be of good courage, and he shall strengthen thine heart: wait, I say, on the LORD.

PSALM 27:14

In whom we have boldness and access with confidence by the faith of him.

EPHESIANS 3:12

For God hath not given us the spirit of fear; but of power, and of love, and of a sound mind.

2 TIMOTHY 1:7

So that we may boldly say, The Lord is my helper, and I will not fear what man shall do unto me.

HEBREWS 13:6

Be of good courage, and he shall strengthen your heart, all ye that hope in the LORD.

PSALM 31:24

The wicked flee when no man pursueth: but the righteous are bold as a lion.

PROVERBS 28:1

Having therefore, brethren, boldness to enter into the holiest by the blood of Jesus.

HEBREWS 10:19

And when the servant of the man of God was risen early, and gone forth, behold, an host compassed the city both with horses and chariots. And his servant said unto him, Alas, my master! how shall we do? And he answered, Fear not: for they that be with us are more than they that be with them.

2 KINGS 6:15–16

Watch ye, stand fast in the faith, quit you like men, be strong.

1 CORINTHIANS 16:13

Only let your conversation be as it becometh the gospel of Christ: that whether I come and see you, or else be absent, I may hear of your affairs, that ye stand fast in one spirit, with one mind striving together for the faith of the gospel; and in nothing terrified by your adversaries: which is to them an evident token of perdition, but to you of salvation, and that of God.

Philippians 1:27–28

And David was greatly distressed; for the people spake of stoning him, because the soul of all the people was grieved, every man for his sons and for his daughters: but David encouraged himself in the Lord his God.

1 Samuel 30:6

And from thence, when the brethren heard of us, they came to meet us as far as Appii forum, and The three taverns: whom when Paul saw, he thanked God, and took courage.

Acts 28:15

Discipline, Family

❧❧❧ ❦❦❦

Fathers, provoke not your children to wrath: but bring them up in the nurture and admonition of the Lord.

EPHESIANS 6:4

Correct thy son, and he shall give thee rest; yea, he shall give delight unto thy soul.

PROVERBS 29:17

He that spareth his rod hateth his son: but he that loveth him chasteneth him betimes.

PROVERBS 13:24

Withhold not correction from the child: for if thou beatest him with the rod, he shall not die. Thou shalt beat him with the rod, and shalt deliver his soul from hell.

PROVERBS 23:13–14

Foolishness is bound in the heart of a child; but the rod of correction shall drive it far from him.

PROVERBS 22:15

Chasten thy son while there is hope, and let not thy soul spare for his crying.

PROVERBS 19:18

Fathers, provoke not your children to anger, lest they be discouraged.

COLOSSIANS 3:21

Even a child is known by his doings, whether his work be pure, and whether it be right.

PROVERBS 20:11

Discipline, God's

⋙ ⋘

Blessed is the man whom thou chastenest, O LORD, and teachest him out of thy law; That thou mayest give him rest from the days of adversity, until the pit be digged for the wicked.

PSALM 94:12–13

Thou shalt also consider in thine heart, that, as a man chasteneth his son, so the LORD thy God chasteneth thee.

DEUTERONOMY 8:5

For if we would judge ourselves, we should not be judged. But when we are judged, we are chastened of the Lord, that we should not be condemned with the world.

1 CORINTHIANS 11:31–32

For the commandment is a lamp; and the law is light; and reproofs of instruction are the way of life.

PROVERBS 6:23

As many as I love, I rebuke and chasten: be zealous therefore, and repent.

REVELATION 3:19

Now no chastening for the present seemeth to be joyous, but grievous: nevertheless afterward it yieldeth the peaceable fruit of righteousness unto them which are exercised thereby.

HEBREWS 12:11

O LORD, rebuke me not in thine anger, neither chasten me in thy hot displeasure.

PSALM 6:1

For whom the LORD loveth he correcteth; even as a father the son in whom he delighteth.

PROVERBS 3:12

Behold, happy is the man whom God correcteth: therefore despise not thou the chastening of the Almighty: For he maketh sore, and bindeth up: he woundeth, and his hands make whole.

JOB 5:17–18

Encouragement

And now I exhort you to be of good cheer: for there shall be no loss of any man's life among you, but of the ship. For there stood by me this night the angel of God, whose I am, and whom I serve, Saying, Fear not, Paul. . .God hath given thee all them that sail with thee.

ACTS 27:22–24

But exhort one another daily, while it is called To day; lest any of you be hardened through the deceitfulness of sin.

HEBREWS 3:13

Holding fast the faithful word as he hath been taught, that he may be able by sound doctrine both to exhort and to convince the gainsayers.

TITUS 1:9

I can do all things through Christ which strengtheneth me.

PHILIPPIANS 4:13

And when they bring you unto the synagogues, and
unto magistrates, and powers, take ye no thought
how or what thing ye shall answer, or what ye shall
say: For the Holy Ghost shall teach you in the same
hour what ye ought to say.

LUKE 12:11–12

Let as many servants as are under the yoke count
their own masters worthy of all honour, that the
name of God and his doctrine be not blasphemed.
And they that have believing masters, let them
not despise them, because they are brethren; but
rather do them service, because they are faithful
and beloved, partakers of the benefit. These things
teach and exhort.

1 TIMOTHY 6:1–2

Brethren, if any of you do err from the truth, and one convert him; Let him know, that he which converteth the sinner from the error of his way shall save a soul from death, and shall hide a multitude of sins.

JAMES 5:19–20

He giveth power to the faint; and to them that have no might he increaseth strength.

ISAIAH 40:29

All scripture is given by inspiration of God, and is profitable for doctrine, for reproof, for correction, for instruction in righteousness.

2 TIMOTHY 3:16

Wherefore comfort yourselves together, and edify one another, even as also ye do.

1 THESSALONIANS 5:11

And whether we be afflicted, it is for your consolation and salvation, which is effectual in the enduring of the same sufferings which we also suffer: or whether we be comforted, it is for your consolation and salvation.

2 CORINTHIANS 1:6

Look not every man on his own things, but every man also on the things of others.

PHILIPPIANS 2:4

Not forsaking the assembling of ourselves together, as the manner of some is; but exhorting one another: and so much the more, as ye see the day approaching.

HEBREWS 10:25

Bear ye one another's burdens, and so fulfil the law of Christ.

GALATIANS 6:2

Eternity

In my Father's house are many mansions: if it were not so, I would have told you. I go to prepare a place for you. And if I go and prepare a place for you, I will come again, and receive you unto myself; that where I am, there ye may be also.

JOHN 14:2–3

Henceforth there is laid up for me a crown of righteousness, which the Lord, the righteous judge, shall give me at that day: and not to me only, but unto all them also that love his appearing.

2 TIMOTHY 4:8

And I saw a new heaven and a new earth: for the first heaven and the first earth were passed away; and there was no more sea. And I John saw the holy city, new Jerusalem, coming down from God out of heaven, prepared as a bride adorned for her husband.

REVELATION 21:1–2

And many of them that sleep in the dust of the earth shall awake, some to everlasting life, and some to shame and everlasting contempt.

DANIEL 12:2

And I give unto them eternal life; and they shall never perish, neither shall any man pluck them out of my hand.

JOHN 10:28

He that loveth his life shall lose it; and he that hateth his life in this world shall keep it unto life eternal.

JOHN 12:25

For the wages of sin is death; but the gift of God is eternal life through Jesus Christ our Lord.

ROMANS 6:23

For we know that if our earthly house of this tabernacle were dissolved, we have a building of God, an house not made with hands, eternal in the heavens.

2 CORINTHIANS 5:1

Behold, I shew you a mystery; We shall not all sleep, but we shall all be changed, In a moment, in the twinkling of an eye, at the last trump: for the trumpet shall sound, and the dead shall be raised incorruptible, and we shall be changed. For this corruptible must put on incorruption, and this mortal must put on immortality. So when this corruptible shall have put on incorruption, and this mortal shall have put on immortality, then shall be brought to pass the saying that is written, Death is swallowed up in victory.

1 Corinthians 15:51–54

Nevertheless we, according to his promise, look for new heavens and a new earth, wherein dwelleth righteousness.

2 Peter 3:13

He that soweth to the Spirit shall of the Spirit reap life everlasting.

Galatians 6:8

And when the chief Shepherd shall appear, ye shall receive a crown of glory that fadeth not away.

1 Peter 5:4

And he saith unto them, Ye shall drink indeed of my cup, and be baptized with the baptism that I am baptized with: but to sit on my right hand, and on my left, is not mine to give, but it shall be given to them for whom it is prepared of my Father.

MATTHEW 20:23

Jesus said unto her, I am the resurrection, and the life: he that believeth in me, though he were dead, yet shall he live: And whosoever liveth and believeth in me shall never die. Believest thou this?

JOHN 11:25–26

Search the scriptures; for in them ye think ye have eternal life: and they are they which testify of me.

JOHN 5:39

God. . .will render to every man according to his deeds: To them who by patient continuance in well doing seek for glory and honour and immortality, eternal life.

ROMANS 2:5–7

And the world passeth away, and the lust thereof: but he that doeth the will of God abideth for ever.

1 JOHN 2:17

But if the Spirit of him that raised up Jesus from the dead dwell in you, he that raised up Christ from the dead shall also quicken your mortal bodies by his Spirit that dwelleth in you.

ROMANS 8:11

And there shall be no night there; and they need no candle, neither light of the sun; for the Lord God giveth them light: and they shall reign for ever and ever.

REVELATION 22:5

Verily, verily, I say unto you, He that heareth my word, and believeth on him that sent me, hath everlasting life, and shall not come into condemnation; but is passed from death unto life.

JOHN 5:24

Faith

Ask in faith, nothing wavering. For he that wavereth is like a wave of the sea driven with the wind and tossed.

JAMES 1:6

Whom having not seen, ye love; in whom, though now ye see him not, yet believing, ye rejoice with joy unspeakable and full of glory.

1 PETER 1:8

And the Lord said, If ye had faith as a grain of mustard seed, ye might say unto this sycamine tree, Be thou plucked up by the root, and be thou planted in the sea; and it should obey you.

LUKE 17:6

As soon as Jesus heard the word that was spoken, he saith unto the ruler of the synagogue, Be not afraid, only believe.

MARK 5:36

And he said to the woman, Thy faith hath saved thee; go in peace.

LUKE 7:50

For ye are all the children of God by faith in Christ Jesus.

GALATIANS 3:26

But as many as received him, to them gave he power to become the sons of God, even to them that believe on his name.

JOHN 1:12

It is written in the prophets, And they shall be all taught of God. Every man therefore that hath heard, and hath learned of the Father, cometh unto me.

JOHN 6:45

He that believeth and is baptized shall be saved; but he that believeth not shall be damned.

MARK 16:16

Now faith is the substance of things hoped for, the evidence of things not seen.

HEBREWS 11:1

That Christ may dwell in your hearts by faith; that ye, being rooted and grounded in love, May be able to comprehend with all saints what is the breadth, and length, and depth, and height; And to know the love of Christ, which passeth knowledge, that ye might be filled with all the fulness of God.

EPHESIANS 3:17–19

Jesus said unto him, If thou canst believe, all things are possible to him that believeth.

MARK 9:23

Watch ye, stand fast in the faith, quit you like men, be strong.

1 CORINTHIANS 16:13

For we walk by faith, not by sight.

2 CORINTHIANS 5:7

That your faith should not stand in the wisdom of men, but in the power of God.

1 Corinthians 2:5

That if thou shalt confess with thy mouth the Lord Jesus, and shalt believe in thine heart that God hath raised him from the dead, thou shalt be saved.

Romans 10:9

And Jesus answering saith unto them, Have faith in God. For verily I say unto you, That whosoever shall say unto this mountain, Be thou removed, and be thou cast into the sea; and shall not doubt in his heart, but shall believe that those things which he saith shall come to pass; he shall have whatsoever he saith.

Mark 11:22–23

Jesus saith unto him, Thomas, because thou hast seen me, thou hast believed: blessed are they that have not seen, and yet have believed.

John 20:29

For by grace are ye saved through faith; and that not of yourselves: it is the gift of God.

EPHESIANS 2:8

Jesus answered and said unto them, This is the work of God, that ye believe on him whom he hath sent.

JOHN 6:29

Jesus saith unto her, Said I not unto thee, that, if thou wouldest believe, thou shouldest see the glory of God?

JOHN 11:40

But without faith it is impossible to please him: for he that cometh to God must believe that he is, and that he is a rewarder of them that diligently seek him.

HEBREWS 11:6

As ye have therefore received Christ Jesus the Lord, so walk ye in him.

COLOSSIANS 2:6–7

Let us draw near with a true heart in full assurance of faith, having our hearts sprinkled from an evil conscience, and our bodies washed with pure water.

HEBREWS 10:22

He that believeth on the Son of God hath the witness in himself: he that believeth not God hath made him a liar; because he believeth not the record that God gave of his Son.

1 JOHN 5:10

The life which I now live in the flesh I live by the faith of the Son of God, who loved me, and gave himself for me.

GALATIANS 2:20

Behold, I stand at the door, and knock: if any man hear my voice, and open the door, I will come in to him, and will sup with him, and he with me.

REVELATION 3:20

Faithfulness of God

And we know that all things work together for good to them that love God, to them who are the called according to his purpose.

ROMANS 8:28

Who then is a faithful and wise servant, whom his lord hath made ruler over his household, to give them meat in due season? Blessed is that servant, whom his lord when he cometh shall find so doing. Verily I say unto you, That he shall make him ruler over all his goods.

MATTHEW 24:45–47

And the heavens shall praise thy wonders, O LORD: thy faithfulness also in the congregation of the saints.

PSALM 89:5

A faithful man shall abound with blessings: but he that maketh haste to be rich shall not be innocent.

PROVERBS 28:20

Therefore thus saith the Lord GOD, Behold, I lay in Zion for a foundation a stone, a tried stone, a precious corner stone, a sure foundation: he that believeth shall not make haste.

ISAIAH 28:16

In hope of eternal life, which God, that cannot lie, promised before the world began.

TITUS 1:2

If we believe not, yet he abideth faithful: he cannot deny himself.

2 TIMOTHY 2:13

The Lord is not slack concerning his promise, as some men count slackness; but is longsuffering to us-ward, not willing that any should perish, but that all should come to repentance.

2 PETER 3:9

Let us hold fast the profession of our faith without wavering; (for he is faithful that promised).

HEBREWS 10:23

Be thou faithful unto death, and I will give thee a crown of life.

REVELATION 2:10

God is not a man, that he should lie; neither the son of man, that he should repent: hath he said, and shall he not do it? or hath he spoken, and shall he not make it good?

NUMBERS 23:19

O love the LORD, all ye his saints: for the LORD preserveth the faithful, and plentifully rewardeth the proud doer.

PSALM 31:23

Know therefore that the LORD thy God, he is God, the faithful God, which keepeth covenant and mercy with them that love him and keep his commandments to a thousand generations.

DEUTERONOMY 7:9

(For the LORD thy God is a merciful God;) he will not forsake thee, neither destroy thee, nor forget the covenant of thy fathers which he sware unto them.

DEUTERONOMY 4:31

Fearing God

The fear of the LORD is the beginning of wisdom: a good understanding have all they that do his commandments: his praise endureth for ever.

PSALM 111:10

Moreover thou shalt provide out of all the people able men, such as fear God, men of truth, hating covetousness; and place such over them, to be rulers of thousands, and rulers of hundreds, rulers of fifties, and rulers of tens.

EXODUS 18:21

Saying with a loud voice, Fear God, and give glory to him; for the hour of his judgment is come; and worship him that made heaven, and earth, and the sea, and the fountains of waters.

REVELATION 14:7

And one of the malefactors which were hanged railed on him, saying, If thou be Christ, save thyself and us. But the other answering rebuked him, saying, Dost not thou fear God, seeing thou art in the same condemnation?

LUKE 23:39–40

But unto you that fear my name shall the Sun of righteousness arise with healing in his wings; and ye shall go forth, and grow up as calves of the stall.

MALACHI 4:2

For in the multitude of dreams and many words there are also divers vanities: but fear thou God.

ECCLESIASTES 5:7

Then Paul stood up, and beckoning with his hand said, Men of Israel, and ye that fear God, give audience. . .to you is the word of this salvation sent.

ACTS 13:16, 26

The fear of the LORD is the beginning of knowledge: but fools despise wisdom and instruction.

PROVERBS 1:7

Submit yourselves to every ordinance of man for the Lord's sake. . . . Honour all men. Love the brotherhood. Fear God. Honour the king.

1 PETER 2:13, 17

Come and hear, all ye that fear God, and I will declare what he hath done for my soul.

PSALM 66:16

Forgiveness

But I say unto you, That ye resist not evil: but whosoever shall smite thee on thy right cheek, turn to him the other also. And if any man will sue thee at the law, and take away thy coat, let him have thy cloak also. And whosoever shall compel thee to go a mile, go with him twain.

MATTHEW 5:39–41

Is any among you afflicted? let him pray. Is any merry? let him sing psalms. Is any sick among you? let him call for the elders of the church; and let them pray over him, anointing him with oil in the name of the Lord: And the prayer of faith shall save the sick, and the Lord shall raise him up; and if he have committed sins, they shall be forgiven him.

JAMES 5:13–15

And be ye kind one to another, tenderhearted, forgiving one another, even as God for Christ's sake hath forgiven you.

EPHESIANS 4:32

If my people, which are called by my name, shall humble themselves, and pray, and seek my face, and turn from their wicked ways; then will I hear from heaven, and will forgive their sin, and will heal their land.

2 Chronicles 7:14

The troubles of my heart are enlarged: O bring thou me out of my distresses. Look upon mine affliction and my pain; and forgive all my sins.

Psalm 25:17–18

If we confess our sins, he is faithful and just to forgive us our sins, and to cleanse us from all unrighteousness. If we say that we have not sinned, we make him a liar, and his word is not in us.

1 John 1:9–10

For thou, Lord, art good, and ready to forgive; and plenteous in mercy unto all them that call upon thee.

Psalm 86:5

Judge not, and ye shall not be judged: condemn not, and ye shall not be condemned: forgive, and ye shall be forgiven.

Luke 6:37

Wherefore I say unto thee, Her sins, which are many, are forgiven; for she loved much: but to whom little is forgiven, the same loveth little. And he said unto her, Thy sins are forgiven.

Luke 7:47–48

And forgive us our debts, as we forgive our debtors.... For if ye forgive men their trespasses, your heavenly Father will also forgive you: But if ye forgive not men their trespasses, neither will your Father forgive your trespasses.

Matthew 6:12, 14–15

Forbearing one another, and forgiving one another, if any man have a quarrel against any: even as Christ forgave you, so also do ye.

COLOSSIANS 3:13

Not rendering evil for evil, or railing for railing: but contrariwise blessing; knowing that ye are thereunto called, that ye should inherit a blessing.

1 PETER 3:9

The discretion of a man deferreth his anger; and it is his glory to pass over a transgression.

PROVERBS 19:11

Then came Peter to him, and said, Lord, how oft shall my brother sin against me, and I forgive him? till seven times? Jesus saith unto him, I say not unto thee, Until seven times: but, Until seventy times seven.

MATTHEW 18:21–22

Take heed to yourselves: If thy brother trespass against thee, rebuke him; and if he repent, forgive him. And if he trespass against thee seven times in a day, and seven times in a day turn again to thee, saying, I repent; thou shalt forgive him.

Luke 17:3–4

And when ye stand praying, forgive, if ye have ought against any: that your Father also which is in heaven may forgive you your trespasses. But if ye do not forgive, neither will your Father which is in heaven forgive your trespasses.

Mark 11:25–26

And forgive us our sins; for we also forgive every one that is indebted to us. And lead us not into temptation; but deliver us from evil.

Luke 11:4

Friendship

My son, if thou be surety for thy friend, if thou hast stricken thy hand with a stranger, Thou art snared with the words of thy mouth, thou art taken with the words of thy mouth.

PROVERBS 6:1–2

Art not thou our God, who didst drive out the inhabitants of this land before thy people Israel, and gavest it to the seed of Abraham thy friend for ever?

2 CHRONICLES 20:7

A man that hath friends must shew himself friendly: and there is a friend that sticketh closer than a brother.

PROVERBS 18:24

Iron sharpeneth iron; so a man sharpeneth the countenance of his friend.

PROVERBS 27:17

A friend loveth at all times.

PROVERBS 17:17

Faithful are the wounds of a friend.

PROVERBS 27:6

Whosoever therefore will be a friend of the world is the enemy of God.

JAMES 4:4

And the Lord talked with Moses. And all the people saw the cloudy pillar stand at the tabernacle door: and all the people rose up and worshipped, every man in his tent door. And the LORD spake unto Moses face to face, as a man speaketh unto his friend.

EXODUS 33:9–11

Generosity

But when thou makest a feast, call the poor, the maimed, the lame, the blind: And thou shalt be blessed; for they cannot recompense thee: for thou shalt be recompensed at the resurrection of the just.

LUKE 14:13–14

Withhold not good from them to whom it is due, when it is in the power of thine hand to do it. Say not unto thy neighbour, Go, and come again, and to morrow I will give; when thou hast it by thee.

PROVERBS 3:27–28

If any of you lack wisdom, let him ask of God, that giveth to all men liberally, and upbraideth not; and it shall be given him.

JAMES 1:5

Charge them that are rich in this world, that they be not highminded, nor trust in uncertain riches, but in the living God, who giveth us richly all things to enjoy; That they do good, that they be rich in good works, ready to distribute, willing to communicate.

1 Timothy 6:17–18

The liberal soul shall be made fat: and he that watereth shall be watered also himself.

Proverbs 11:25

Upon the first day of the week let every one of you lay by him in store, as God hath prospered him, that there be no gatherings when I come. And when I come, whomsoever ye shall approve by your letters, them will I send to bring your liberality unto Jerusalem.

1 Corinthians 16:2–3

He hath dispersed, he hath given to the poor; his righteousness endureth for ever; his horn shall be exalted with honour.

PSALM 112:9

And if thy brother, an Hebrew man, or an Hebrew woman, be sold unto thee, and serve thee six years; then in the seventh year thou shalt let him go free from thee. And when thou sendest him out free from thee, thou shalt not let him go away empty: Thou shalt furnish him liberally out of thy flock, and out of thy floor, and out of thy winepress: of that wherewith the LORD thy God hath blessed thee thou shalt give unto him.

DEUTERONOMY 15:12–14

He that despiseth his neighbour sinneth: but he that hath mercy on the poor, happy is he.

PROVERBS 14:21

And if thy brother be waxen poor, and fallen in decay with thee; then thou shalt relieve him: yea, though he be a stranger, or a sojourner; that he may live with thee.

Leviticus 25:35

Therefore when thou doest thine alms, do not sound a trumpet before thee, as the hypocrites do in the synagogues and in the streets, that they may have glory of men. Verily I say unto you, They have their reward. But when thou doest alms, let not thy left hand know what thy right hand doeth: That thine alms may be in secret: and thy Father which seeth in secret himself shall reward thee openly.

Matthew 6:2–4

He answereth and saith unto them, He that hath two coats, let him impart to him that hath none; and he that hath meat, let him do likewise.

Luke 3:11

And he saw also a certain poor widow casting in thither two mites. And he said, Of a truth I say unto you, that this poor widow hath cast in more than they all: For all these have of their abundance cast in unto the offerings of God: but she of her penury hath cast in all the living that she had.

LUKE 21:2–4

If any man or woman that believeth have widows, let them relieve them, and let not the church be charged; that it may relieve them that are widows indeed.

1 TIMOTHY 5:16

For the poor shall never cease out of the land: therefore I command thee, saying, Thou shalt open thine hand wide unto thy brother, to thy poor, and to thy needy, in thy land.

DEUTERONOMY 15:11

Moreover, brethren, we do you to wit of the grace of God bestowed on the churches of Macedonia; How that in a great trial of affliction the abundance of their joy and their deep poverty abounded unto the riches of their liberality. . . . Every man according as he purposeth in his heart, so let him give; not grudgingly, or of necessity: for God loveth a cheerful giver.

2 Corinthians 8:1–2; 9:7

Every man shall give as he is able, according to the blessing of the Lord thy God which he hath given thee.

Deuteronomy 16:17

Give, and it shall be given unto you; good measure, pressed down, and shaken together, and running over, shall men give into your bosom. For with the same measure that ye mete withal it shall be measured to you again.

Luke 6:38

Then shall the King say unto them on his right hand, Come, ye blessed of my Father, inherit the kingdom prepared for you from the foundation of the world: For I was an hungred, and ye gave me meat: I was thirsty, and ye gave me drink: I was a stranger, and ye took me in: Naked, and ye clothed me: I was sick, and ye visited me: I was in prison, and ye came unto me. Then shall the righteous answer him, saying, Lord, when saw we thee an hungred, and fed thee? or thirsty, and gave thee drink? When saw we thee a stranger, and took thee in? or naked, and clothed thee? Or when saw we thee sick, or in prison, and came unto thee? And the King shall answer and say unto them, Verily I say unto you, Inasmuch as ye have done it unto one of the least of these my brethren, ye have done it unto me.

MATTHEW 25:34–40

Every man according as he purposeth in his heart, so let him give; not grudgingly, or of necessity: for God loveth a cheerful giver.

2 CORINTHIANS 9:7

He that hath pity upon the poor lendeth unto the LORD; and that which he hath given will he pay him again.

PROVERBS 19:17

Is it not to deal thy bread to the hungry, and that thou bring the poor that are cast out to thy house? when thou seest the naked, that thou cover him; and that thou hide not thyself from thine own flesh? Then shall thy light break forth as the morning, and thine health shall spring forth speedily: and thy righteousness shall go before thee; the glory of the LORD shall be thy rereward.

ISAIAH 58:7–8

For whosoever shall give you a cup of water to drink in my name, because ye belong to Christ, verily I say unto you, he shall not lose his reward.

MARK 9:41

I have shewed you all things, how that so labouring ye ought to support the weak, and to remember the words of the Lord Jesus, how he said, It is more blessed to give than to receive.

ACTS 20:35

Blessed is he that considereth the poor: the LORD will deliver him in time of trouble. The LORD will preserve him, and keep him alive; and he shall be blessed upon the earth: and thou wilt not deliver him unto the will of his enemies.

PSALM 41:1–2

For ye know the grace of our Lord Jesus Christ, that, though he was rich, yet for your sakes he became poor, that ye through his poverty might be rich.

2 CORINTHIANS 8:9

Gentleness

He shall feed his flock like a shepherd: he shall gather the lambs with his arm, and carry them in his bosom, and shall gently lead those that are with young.

Isaiah 40:11

Now I Paul myself beseech you by the meekness and gentleness of Christ, who in presence am base among you, but being absent am bold toward you. . . . For though we walk in the flesh, we do not war after the flesh.

2 Corinthians 10:1, 3

And the king commanded Joab and Abishai and Ittai, saying, Deal gently for my sake with the young man, even with Absalom.

2 Samuel 18:5

For the Lord taketh pleasure in his people: he will beautify the meek with salvation.

Psalm 149:4

Thou hast also given me the shield of thy salvation: and thy gentleness hath made me great.

2 SAMUEL 22:36

But we were gentle among you, even as a nurse cherisheth her children: So being affectionately desirous of you, we were willing to have imparted unto you, not the gospel of God only, but also our own souls.

1 THESSALONIANS 2:7–8

But the wisdom that is from above is first pure, then peaceable, gentle, and easy to be intreated, full of mercy and good fruits, without partiality, and without hypocrisy. And the fruit of righteousness is sown in peace of them that make peace.

JAMES 3:17–18

The meek shall eat and be satisfied: they shall praise the LORD that seek him: your heart shall live for ever.

PSALM 22:26

To speak evil of no man, to be no brawlers, but gentle, shewing all meekness unto all men. For we ourselves also were sometimes foolish. . . . That being justified by his grace, we should be made heirs according to the hope of eternal life.

Titus 3:2–3, 7

But the fruit of the Spirit is love, joy, peace, longsuffering, gentleness, goodness, faith, Meekness, temperance: against such there is no law.

Galatians 5:22–23

Take my yoke upon you, and learn of me; for I am meek and lowly in heart: and ye shall find rest unto your souls.

Matthew 11:29

The Lord lifteth up the meek: he casteth the wicked down to the ground.

Psalm 147:6

But the wisdom that is from above is first pure, then peaceable, gentle, and easy to be intreated, full of mercy and good fruits, without partiality, and without hypocrisy.

JAMES 3:17

But the meek shall inherit the earth; and shall delight themselves in the abundance of peace.

PSALM 37:11

The meek will he guide in judgment: and the meek will he teach his way.

PSALM 25:9

And the servant of the Lord must not strive; but be gentle unto all men, apt to teach, patient, In meekness instructing those that oppose themselves; if God peradventure will give them repentance to the acknowledging of the truth; And that they may recover themselves out of the snare of the devil, who are taken captive by him at his will.

2 TIMOTHY 2:24–26

God's Love

Behold, what manner of love the Father hath bestowed upon us, that we should be called the sons of God.

1 JOHN 3:1

In this was manifested the love of God toward us, because that God sent his only begotten Son into the world, that we might live through him.

1 JOHN 4:9

I will heal their backsliding, I will love them freely: for mine anger is turned away from him.

HOSEA 14:4

But God commendeth his love toward us, in that, while we were yet sinners, Christ died for us.

ROMANS 5:8

Herein is love, not that we loved God, but that he loved us, and sent his Son to be the propitiation for our sins.

1 John 4:10

But as it is written, Eye hath not seen, nor ear heard, neither have entered into the heart of man, the things which God hath prepared for them that love him.

1 Corinthians 2:9

For I am persuaded, that neither death, nor life, nor angels, nor principalities, nor powers, nor things present, nor things to come, nor height, nor depth, nor any other creature, shall be able to separate us from the love of God, which is in Christ Jesus our Lord.

Romans 8:38–39

The Lord preserveth all them that love him.

Psalm 145:20

And hope maketh not ashamed; because the love of God is shed abroad in our hearts by the Holy Ghost which is given unto us.

ROMANS 5:5

And we have known and believed the love that God hath to us. God is love; and he that dwelleth in love dwelleth in God, and God in him.

1 JOHN 4:16

For God so loved the world, that he gave his only begotten Son, that whosoever believeth in him should not perish, but have everlasting life.

JOHN 3:16

For the Father himself loveth you, because ye have loved me, and have believed that I came out from God.

JOHN 16:27

God's Provision

❧⟫⟫ ⟪⟪❧

These twelve Jesus sent forth, and commanded them, saying, Go not into the way of the Gentiles, and into any city of the Samaritans enter ye not: But go rather to the lost sheep of the house of Israel. . . . Provide neither gold, nor silver, nor brass in your purses, Nor scrip for your journey, neither two coats, neither shoes, nor yet staves: for the workman is worthy of his meat.

MATTHEW 10:5–6, 9–10

And these all, having obtained a good report through faith, received not the promise: God having provided some better thing for us, that they without us should not be made perfect.

HEBREWS 11:39–40

But my God shall supply all your need according to his riches in glory by Christ Jesus.

PHILIPPIANS 4:19

Charge them that are rich in this world, that they be not highminded, nor trust in uncertain riches, but in the living God, who giveth us richly all things to enjoy.

1 Timothy 6:17

Recompense to no man evil for evil. Provide things honest in the sight of all men. If it be possible, as much as lieth in you, live peaceably with all men. Dearly beloved, avenge not yourselves, but rather give place unto wrath: for it is written, Vengeance is mine; I will repay, saith the Lord. . . . Be not overcome of evil, but overcome evil with good.

Romans 12:17–19, 21

Sell that ye have, and give alms; provide yourselves bags which wax not old, a treasure in the heavens that faileth not, where no thief approacheth, neither moth corrupteth. For where your treasure is, there will your heart be also.

Luke 12:33–34

Therefore I say unto you, Take no thought for your life, what ye shall eat, or what ye shall drink; nor yet for your body, what ye shall put on. Is not the life more than meat, and the body than raiment? Behold the fowls of the air: for they sow not, neither do they reap, nor gather into barns; yet your heavenly Father feedeth them. Are ye not much better than they? Which of you by taking thought can add one cubit unto his stature? And why take ye thought for raiment? Consider the lilies of the field, how they grow; they toil not, neither do they spin: And yet I say unto you, That even Solomon in all his glory was not arrayed like one of these. Wherefore, if God so clothe the grass of the field, which to day is, and to morrow is cast into the oven, shall he not much more clothe you, O ye of little faith? Therefore take no thought, saying, What shall we eat? or, What shall we drink? or, Wherewithal shall we be clothed? (For after all these things do the Gentiles seek:) for your heavenly Father knoweth that ye have need of all these things. But seek ye first the kingdom of God, and his righteousness; and all these things shall be added unto you.

MATTHEW 6:25–33

And Isaac spake unto Abraham his father, and said, My father: and he said, Here am I, my son. And he said, Behold the fire and the wood: but where is the lamb for a burnt offering? And Abraham said, My son, God will provide himself a lamb for a burnt offering: so they went both of them together.

GENESIS 22:7–8

The young lions do lack, and suffer hunger: but they that seek the LORD shall not want any good thing.

PSALM 34:10

He hath given meat unto them that fear him.

PSALM 111:5

Graciousness

And therefore will the LORD wait, that he may be gracious unto you, and therefore will he be exalted, that he may have mercy upon you. . . . Thou shalt weep no more: he will be very gracious unto thee at the voice of thy cry; when he shall hear it, he will answer thee.

ISAIAH 30:18–19

The LORD bless thee, and keep thee: The LORD make his face shine upon thee, and be gracious unto thee: The LORD lift up his countenance upon thee, and give thee peace.

NUMBERS 6:24–26

A gracious woman retaineth honour: and strong men retain riches.

PROVERBS 11:16

And there was delivered unto him the book of the prophet Esaias. And when he had opened the book, he found the place where it was written, the Spirit of the Lord is upon me, because he hath anointed me. . .To preach the acceptable year of the Lord. And he closed the book. . . . And he began to say unto them, This day is this scripture fulfilled in your ears. And all. . .wondered at the gracious words which proceeded out of his mouth.

LUKE 4:17–22

But thou, O Lord, art a God full of compassion, and gracious, long suffering, and plenteous in mercy and truth.

PSALM 86:15

92

Wherefore laying aside all malice, and all guile, and hypocrisies, and envies, and all evil speakings, As newborn babes, desire the sincere milk of the word, that ye may grow thereby: If so be ye have tasted that the Lord is gracious.

1 Peter 2:1–3

And he prayed unto the Lord, and said, I pray thee, O Lord, was not this my saying, when I was yet in my country? Therefore I fled before unto Tarshish: for I knew that thou art a gracious God, and merciful, slow to anger, and of great kindness, and repentest thee of the evil.

Jonah 4:2

Gratitude

And he took the cup, and gave thanks, and gave it to them, saying, Drink ye all of it.

MATTHEW 26:27

That I may publish with the voice of thanksgiving, and tell of all thy wondrous works.

PSALM 26:7

Giving thanks always for all things unto God and the Father in the name of our Lord Jesus Christ.

EPHESIANS 5:20

I will mention the lovingkindnesses of the LORD, and the praises of the LORD, according to all that the LORD hath bestowed on us, and the great goodness toward the house of Israel, which he hath bestowed on them according to his mercies, and according to the multitude of his lovingkindnesses.

ISAIAH 63:7

Blessed be the LORD, that hath given rest unto his people Israel, according to all that he promised: there hath not failed one word of all his good promise, which he promised by the hand of Moses his servant.

1 KINGS 8:56

O LORD, thou hast brought up my soul from the grave: thou hast kept me alive, that I should not go down to the pit.

PSALM 30:3

In every thing give thanks: for this is the will of God in Christ Jesus concerning you.

1 THESSALONIANS 5:18

O give thanks unto the LORD; for he is good: for his mercy endureth for ever.

PSALM 136:1

And he took the seven loaves and the fishes, and gave thanks, and brake them, and gave to his disciples, and the disciples to the multitude.

MATTHEW 15:36

I will praise thee, O LORD, with my whole heart; I will shew forth all thy marvellous works. I will be glad and rejoice in thee: I will sing praise to thy name, O thou most High.

PSALM 9:1–2

Thou hast turned for me my mourning into dancing: thou hast put off my sackcloth, and girded me with gladness; To the end that my glory may sing praise to thee, and not be silent. O LORD my God, I will give thanks unto thee for ever.

PSALM 30:11–12

It is a good thing to give thanks unto the LORD, and to sing praises unto thy name, O most High: To shew forth thy lovingkindness in the morning, and thy faithfulness every night.

PSALM 92:1–2

He that regardeth the day, regardeth it unto the Lord; and he that regardeth not the day, to the Lord he doth not regard it. He that eateth, eateth to the Lord, for he giveth God thanks; and he that eateth not, to the Lord he eateth not, and giveth God thanks.

ROMANS 14:6

I thank thee, and praise thee, O thou God of my fathers, who hast given me wisdom and might, and hast made known unto me now what we desired of thee: for thou hast now made known unto us the king's matter.

DANIEL 2:23

And they, continuing daily with one accord in the temple, and breaking bread from house to house, did eat their meat with gladness and singleness of heart, Praising God, and having favour with all the people. And the Lord added to the church daily such as should be saved.

Acts 2:46–47

Many, O Lord my God, are thy wonderful works which thou hast done, and thy thoughts which are to us-ward: they cannot be reckoned up in order unto thee: if I would declare and speak of them, they are more than can be numbered.

Psalm 40:5

Blessed be the Lord, who daily loadeth us with benefits, even the God of our salvation. Selah.

Psalm 68:19

Honesty

And that ye study to be quiet, and to do your own business, and to work with your own hands. . . . That ye may walk honestly toward them that are without, and that ye may have lack of nothing.

1 THESSALONIANS 4:11–12

I exhort therefore, that, first of all, supplications, prayers, intercessions, and giving of thanks, be made for all men; For kings, and for all that are in authority; that we may lead a quiet and peaceable life in all godliness and honesty. For this is good and acceptable in the sight of God our Saviour.

1 TIMOTHY 2:1–3

Finally, brethren, whatsoever things are true, whatsoever things are honest, whatsoever things are just, whatsoever things are pure, whatsoever things are lovely, whatsoever things are of good report; if there be any virtue, and if there be any praise, think on these things.

PHILIPPIANS 4:8

A sower went out to sow his seed: and as he sowed, some fell by the way side; and it was trodden down, and the fowls of the air devoured it. . . . And other fell on good ground, and sprang up, and bare fruit an hundredfold. . . . But that on the good ground are they, which in an honest and good heart, having heard the word, keep it, and bring forth fruit with patience.

LUKE 8:5, 8, 15

The night is far spent, the day is at hand: let us therefore cast off the works of darkness, and let us put on the armour of light. Let us walk honestly, as in the day; not in rioting and drunkenness, not in chambering and wantonness, not in strife and envying.

ROMANS 13:12–13

And herein do I exercise myself, to have always a conscience void of offence toward God, and toward men.

ACTS 24:16

Pray for us: for we trust we have a good conscience, in all things willing to live honestly.

HEBREWS 13:18

Thou knowest the commandments, Do not commit adultery, Do not kill, Do not steal, Do not bear false witness.

MARK 10:19

Be of the same mind one toward another. . . . Recompense to no man evil for evil. Provide things honest in the sight of all men.

ROMANS 12:16–17

Servants, obey in all things your masters according to the flesh; not with eyeservice, as menpleasers; but in singleness of heart, fearing God.

COLOSSIANS 3:22

Ye shall not steal, neither deal falsely, neither lie one to another.

LEVITICUS 19:11

He that putteth not out his money to usury, nor taketh reward against the innocent. He that doeth these things shall never be moved.

PSALM 15:5

And as ye would that men should do to you, do ye also to them likewise.

LUKE 6:31

Therefore all things whatsoever ye would that men should do to you, do ye even so to them: for this is the law and the prophets.

MATTHEW 7:12

Lie not one to another, seeing that ye have put off the old man with his deeds; And have put on the new man, which is renewed in knowledge after the image of him that created him.

COLOSSIANS 3:9–10

Providing for honest things, not only in the sight of the Lord, but also in the sight of men.

2 CORINTHIANS 8:21

He that walketh righteously, and speaketh uprightly; he that despiseth the gain of oppressions, that shaketh his hands from holding of bribes, that stoppeth his ears from hearing of blood, and shutteth his eyes from seeing evil; He shall dwell on high: his place of defence shall be the munitions of rocks: bread shall be given him; his waters shall be sure.

ISAIAH 33:15–16

Then came also publicans to be baptized, and said unto him, Master, what shall we do? And he said unto them, Exact no more than that which is appointed you.

LUKE 3:12–13

He that hath clean hands, and a pure heart; who hath not lifted up his soul unto vanity, nor sworn deceitfully.

PSALM 24:4

Receive us; we have wronged no man, we have corrupted no man, we have defrauded no man.

2 CORINTHIANS 7:2

Honor

Honour thy father and thy mother: that thy days may be long upon the land which the LORD thy God giveth thee.

EXODUS 20:12

Honour the LORD with thy substance, and with the firstfruits of all thine increase: So shall thy barns be filled with plenty, and thy presses shall burst out with new wine.

PROVERBS 3:9–10

Children, obey your parents in the Lord: for this is right. Honour thy father and mother; which is the first commandment with promise; That it may be well with thee, and thou mayest live long on the earth.

EPHESIANS 6:1–3

If any man serve me, let him follow me; and where I am, there shall also my servant be: if any man serve me, him will my Father honour.

JOHN 12:26

Thy throne, O God, is for ever and ever: the sceptre of thy kingdom is a right sceptre. . . . Kings' daughters were among thy honourable women: upon thy right hand did stand the queen in gold of Ophir. . . . So shall the king greatly desire thy beauty: for he is thy Lord.

PSALM 45:6, 9, 11

That all men should honour the Son, even as they honour the Father. He that honoureth not the Son honoureth not the Father which hath sent him.

JOHN 5:23

Happy is the man that findeth wisdom, and the man that getteth understanding. . . . She is more precious than rubies: and all the things thou canst desire are not to be compared unto her. Length of days is in her right hand; and in her left hand riches and honour.

PROVERBS 3:13, 15–16

If thou turn away thy foot from the sabbath, from doing thy pleasure on my holy day; and call the sabbath a delight, the holy of the LORD, honourable; and shalt honour him, not doing thine own ways, nor finding thine own pleasure, nor speaking thine own words: Then shalt thou delight thyself in the LORD; and I will cause thee to ride upon the high places of the earth, and feed thee with the heritage of Jacob thy father: for the mouth of the LORD hath spoken it.

ISAIAH 58:13–14

And the brethren immediately sent away Paul and Silas by night unto Berea. . . . They received the word with all readiness of mind, and searched the scriptures daily, whether those things were so. Therefore many of them believed; also of honourable women which were Greeks, and of men, not a few.

ACTS 17:10–12

And those members of the body, which we think to be less honourable, upon these we bestow more abundant honour; and our uncomely parts have more abundant comeliness.

1 CORINTHIANS 12:23

Marriage is honourable in all, and the bed undefiled: but whoremongers and adulterers God will judge.

HEBREWS 13:4

Hope

But let us, who are of the day, be sober, putting on the breastplate of faith and love; and for an helmet, the hope of salvation.

1 Thessalonians 5:8

The hope of the righteous shall be gladness: but the expectation of the wicked shall perish.

Proverbs 10:28

Beloved, now are we the sons of God, and it doth not yet appear what we shall be: but we know that, when he shall appear, we shall be like him; for we shall see him as he is. And every man that hath this hope in him purifieth himself, even as he is pure.

1 John 3:2–3

And not only so, but we glory in tribulations also: knowing that tribulation worketh patience; and patience, experience; and experience, hope: And hope maketh not ashamed.

Romans 5:3–5

Blessed be the God and Father of our Lord Jesus Christ, which according to his abundant mercy hath begotten us again unto a lively hope by the resurrection of Jesus Christ from the dead.

1 Peter 1:3

But sanctify the Lord God in your hearts: and be ready always to give an answer to every man that asketh you a reason of the hope that is in you with meekness and fear.

1 Peter 3:15

But I would not have you to be ignorant, brethren, concerning them which are asleep, that ye sorrow not, even as others which have no hope. For if we believe that Jesus died and rose again, even so them also which sleep in Jesus will God bring with him.

1 Thessalonians 4:13–14

The Lord is my portion, saith my soul; therefore will I hope in him. The Lord is good unto them that wait for him, to the soul that seeketh him. It is good that a man should both hope and quietly wait for the salvation of the Lord.

LAMENTATIONS 3:24–26

The wicked is driven away in his wickedness: but the righteous hath hope in his death.

PROVERBS 14:32

Remember thy word unto thy servant, upon which thou hast caused me to hope. . . . My soul fainteth for thy salvation: but I hope in thy word. . . . Thou art my hiding place and my shield: I hope in thy word.

PSALM 119:49, 81, 114

For we through the Spirit wait for the hope of righteousness by faith.

GALATIANS 5:5

Blessed is the man that trusteth in the LORD, and whose hope the LORD is.

JEREMIAH 17:7

For the grace of God that bringeth salvation hath appeared to all men, Teaching us that. . .we should live soberly, righteously, and godly, in this present world; Looking for that blessed hope, and the glorious appearing of the great God and our Saviour Jesus Christ.

TITUS 2:11–13

And we desire that every one of you do shew the same diligence to the full assurance of hope unto the end: That ye be not slothful, but followers of them who through faith and patience inherit the promises.

HEBREWS 6:11–12

Chasten thy son while there is hope, and let not thy soul spare for his crying.

PROVERBS 19:18

In hope of eternal life, which God, that cannot lie, promised before the world began.

TITUS 1:2

But Christ as a son over his own house; whose house are we, if we hold fast the confidence and the rejoicing of the hope firm unto the end.

HEBREWS 3:6

That by two immutable things, in which it was impossible for God to lie, we might have a strong consolation, who have fled for refuge to lay hold upon the hope set before us: Which hope we have as an anchor of the soul, both sure and stedfast, and which entereth into that within the veil.

HEBREWS 6:18–19

Now the God of hope fill you with all joy and peace in believing, that ye may abound in hope, through the power of the Holy Ghost.

ROMANS 15:13

To whom God would make known what is the riches of the glory of this mystery among the Gentiles; which is Christ in you, the hope of glory.

COLOSSIANS 1:27

But I will hope continually, and will yet praise thee more and more.

PSALM 71:14

Who by him do believe in God, that raised him up from the dead, and gave him glory; that your faith and hope might be in God.

1 PETER 1:21

And have hope toward God, which they themselves also allow, that there shall be a resurrection of the dead, both of the just and unjust.

ACTS 24:15

And we desire that every one of you do shew the same diligence to the full assurance of hope unto the end.

HEBREWS 6:11

Who against hope believed in hope, that he might become the father of many nations, according to that which was spoken, So shall thy seed be.

ROMANS 4:18

There is one body, and one Spirit, even as ye are called in one hope of your calling.

EPHESIANS 4:4

For we are saved by hope: but hope that is seen is not hope: for what a man seeth, why doth he yet hope for? But if we hope for that we see not, then do we with patience wait for it.

ROMANS 8:24–25

LORD, I have hoped for thy salvation, and done thy commandments.

PSALM 119:166

Seeing then that we have such hope, we use great plainness of speech.

2 CORINTHIANS 3:12

The eyes of your understanding being enlightened; that ye may know what is the hope of his calling, and what the riches of the glory of his inheritance in the saints.

EPHESIANS 1:18

For the hope which is laid up for you in heaven, whereof ye heard before in the word of the truth of the gospel.

COLOSSIANS 1:5

Now faith is the substance of things hoped for, the evidence of things not seen.

HEBREWS 11:1

According to my earnest expectation and my hope, that in nothing I shall be ashamed, but that with all boldness, as always, so now also Christ shall be magnified in my body, whether it be by life, or by death.

PHILIPPIANS 1:20

Remember the word unto thy servant, upon which thou hast caused me to hope.

PSALM 119:49

Why art thou cast down, O my soul? and why art thou disquieted within me? hope thou in God: for I shall yet praise him, who is the health of my countenance, and my God.

PSALM 42:11

For the needy shall not alway be forgotten: the expectation of the poor shall not perish for ever.

PSALM 9:18

Hospitality

And above all things have fervent charity among yourselves: for charity shall cover the multitude of sins. Use hospitality one to another without grudging. As every man hath received the gift, even so minister the same one to another, as good stewards of the manifold grace of God.

1 Peter 4:8–10

Then shall the King say unto them on his right hand, Come, ye blessed of my Father, inherit the kingdom prepared for you from the foundation of the world: For I was an hungred, and ye gave me meat: I was thirsty, and ye gave me drink: I was a stranger, and ye took me in: Naked, and ye clothed me: I was sick, and ye visited me: I was in prison, and ye came unto me. . . . And the King shall answer and say unto them, Verily I say unto you, Inasmuch as ye have done it unto one of the least of these my brethren, ye have done it unto me.

Matthew 25:34–36, 40

If a brother or sister be naked, and destitute of daily food, And one of you say unto them, Depart in peace, be ye warmed and filled; notwithstanding ye give them not those things which are needful to the body; what doth it profit? . . . But wilt thou know, O vain man, that faith without works is dead? . . . Ye see then how that by works a man is justified, and not by faith only.

JAMES 2:15–16, 20, 24

Rejoicing in hope; patient in tribulation; continuing instant in prayer; Distributing to the necessity of saints; given to hospitality.

ROMANS 12:12–13

I have shewed you all things, how that so labouring ye ought to support the weak, and to remember the words of the Lord Jesus, how he said, It is more blessed to give than to receive.

ACTS 20:35

For a bishop must be blameless, as the steward of God; not selfwilled, not soon angry. . .But a lover of hospitality, a lover of good men, sober, just, holy, temperate.

Titus 1:7–8

For ye know the grace of our Lord Jesus Christ, that, though he was rich, yet for your sakes he became poor, that ye through his poverty might be rich. . . . But by an equality, that now at this time your abundance may be a supply for their want, that their abundance also may be a supply for your want: that there may be equality: As it is written, He that had gathered much had nothing over; and he that had gathered little had no lack.

2 Corinthians 8:9, 14–15

But whoso hath this world's good, and seeth his brother have need, and shutteth up his bowels of compassion from him, how dwelleth the love of God in him? My little children, let us not love in word, neither in tongue; but in deed and in truth.

1 John 3:17–18

And if a stranger sojourn with thee in your land, ye shall not vex him. But the stranger that dwelleth with you shall be unto you as one born among you, and thou shalt love him as thyself.

LEVITICUS 19:33–34

But when thou makest a feast, call the poor, the maimed, the lame, the blind: And thou shalt be blessed; for they cannot recompense thee: for thou shalt be recompensed at the resurrection of the just.

LUKE 14:13–14

Well reported of for good works; if she have brought up children, if she have lodged strangers, if she have washed the saints' feet, if she have relieved the afflicted, if she have diligently followed every good work.

1 TIMOTHY 5:10

He doth execute the judgment of the fatherless and widow, and loveth the stranger, in giving him food and rainment.

DEUTERONOMY 10:18

And thou shalt not glean thy vineyard, neither shalt thou gather every grape of thy vineyard; thou shalt leave them for the poor and stranger: I am the LORD your God.

LEVITICUS 19:10

Wisdom hath builded her house, she hath hewn out her seven pillars: She hath killed her beasts; she hath mingled her wine; she hath also furnished her table. She hath sent forth her maidens: she crieth upon the highest places of the city, Whoso is simple, let him turn in hither: as for him that wanteth understanding, she saith to him, Come, eat of my bread, and drink of the wine which I have mingled.

PROVERBS 9:1–5

Distributing to the necessity of saints; given to hospitality.

ROMANS 12:13

For whosoever shall give you a cup of water to drink in my name, because ye belong to Christ, verily I say unto you, he shall not lose his reward.

MARK 9:41

Let brotherly love continue. Be not forgetful to entertain strangers: for thereby some have entertained angels unawares.

HEBREWS 13:1–2

Humility

Boast not thyself of to morrow; for thou knowest not what a day may bring forth.

PROVERBS 27:1

Thus saith the LORD, Let not the wise man glory in his wisdom, neither let the mighty man glory in his might, let not the rich man glory in his riches.

JEREMIAH 9:23

If I must needs glory, I will glory of the things which concern mine infirmities.

2 CORINTHIANS 11:30

Hearken to me, ye that follow after righteousness, ye that seek the LORD: look unto the rock whence ye are hewn, and to the hole of the pit whence ye are digged.

ISAIAH 51:1

Be not wise in your own conceits.

ROMANS 12:16

Lord, my heart is not haughty, nor mine eyes lofty: neither do I exercise myself in great matters, or in things too high for me.

PSALM 131:1

Yea, all of you be subject one to another, and be clothed with humility: for God resisteth the proud, and giveth grace to the humble. Humble yourselves therefore under the mighty hand of God, that he may exalt you in due time.

1 PETER 5:5–6

The fear of the LORD is the instruction of wisdom; and before honour is humility.

PROVERBS 15:33

By humility and the fear of the LORD are riches, and honour, and life.

PROVERBS 22:4

Blessed are the poor in spirit: for theirs is the kingdom of heaven.

Matthew 5:3

Lord, thou hast heard the desire of the humble: thou wilt prepare their heart, thou wilt cause thine ear to hear.

Psalm 10:17

When men are cast down, then thou shalt say, There is lifting up; and he shall save the humble person.

Job 22:29

Whosoever therefore shall humble himself as this little child, the same is greatest in the kingdom of heaven.

Matthew 18:4

Surely he scorneth the scorners: but he giveth grace unto the lowly.

Proverbs 3:34

And whosoever shall exalt himself shall be abased; and he that shall humble himself shall be exalted.

Matthew 23:12

Though the Lord be high, yet hath he respect unto the lowly: but the proud he knoweth afar off.

Psalm 138:6

For thus saith the high and lofty One that inhabiteth eternity, whose name is Holy; I dwell in the high and holy place, with him also that is of a contrite and humble spirit, to revive the spirit of the humble, and to revive the heart of the contrite ones.

Isaiah 57:15

But made himself of no reputation, and took upon him the form of a servant, and was made in the likeness of men: And being found in fashion as a man, he humbled himself, and became obedient unto death, even the death of the cross. Wherefore God also hath highly exalted him, and given him a name which is above every name.

Philippians 2:7–9

When pride cometh, then cometh shame: but with the lowly is wisdom.

PROVERBS 11:2

When he maketh inquisition for blood, he remembereth them: he forgetteth not the cry of the humble.

PSALM 9:12

Humble yourselves in the sight of the Lord, and he shall lift you up.

JAMES 4:10

Behold even to the moon, and it shineth not; yea, the stars are not pure in his sight. How much less man, that is a worm? and the son of man, which is a worm?

JOB 25:5–6

Better it is to be of an humble spirit with the lowly, than to divide the spoil with the proud.

PROVERBS 16:19

Joy

And the angel said unto them, Fear not: for, behold, I bring you good tidings of great joy, which shall be to all people.

LUKE 2:10

The LORD is my strength and my shield; my heart trusted in him, and I am helped: therefore my heart greatly rejoiceth; and with my song will I praise him.

PSALM 28:7

Rejoice in the Lord alway: and again I say, Rejoice.

PHILIPPIANS 4:4

Hitherto have ye asked nothing in my name: ask, and ye shall receive, that your joy may be full.

JOHN 16:24

Be glad in the LORD, and rejoice, ye righteous: and shout for joy, all ye that are upright in heart.

PSALM 32:11

In the transgression of an evil man there is a snare: but the righteous doth sing and rejoice.

PROVERBS 29:6

As sorrowful, yet alway rejoicing; as poor, yet making many rich; as having nothing, and yet possessing all things.

2 CORINTHIANS 6:10

My lips shall greatly rejoice when I sing unto thee; and my soul, which thou hast redeemed.

PSALM 71:23

Rejoice ye in that day, and leap for joy: for, behold, your reward is great in heaven: for in the like manner did their fathers unto the prophets.

LUKE 6:23

A merry heart doeth good like a medicine.

PROVERBS 17:22

Therefore the redeemed of the Lord shall return, and come with singing unto Zion; and everlasting joy shall be upon their head: they shall obtain gladness and joy; and sorrow and mourning shall flee away.

Isaiah 51:11

His lord said unto him, Well done, thou good and faithful servant: thou hast been faithful over a few things, I will make thee ruler over many things: enter thou into the joy of thy lord.

Matthew 25:21

Make a joyful noise unto the Lord, all ye lands. Serve the Lord with gladness: come before his presence with singing.

Psalm 100:1–2

And now come I to thee; and these things I speak in the world, that they might have my joy fulfilled in themselves.

John 17:13

All the days of the afflicted are evil: but he that is of a merry heart hath a continual feast.

PROVERBS 15:15

Let all those that seek thee rejoice and be glad in thee: let such as love thy salvation say continually, The LORD be magnified.

PSALM 40:16

And not only so, but we also joy in God through our Lord Jesus Christ, by whom we have now received the atonement.

ROMANS 5:11

Not for that we have dominion over your faith, but are helpers of your joy: for by faith ye stand.

2 CORINTHIANS 1:24

For our heart shall rejoice in him, because we have trusted in his holy name.

PSALM 33:21

I will greatly rejoice in the LORD, my soul shall be joyful in my God; for he hath clothed me with the garments of salvation, he hath covered me with the robe of righteousness, as a bridegroom decketh himself with ornaments, and as a bride adorneth herself with her jewels.

ISAIAH 61:10

Is any merry? let him sing psalms.

JAMES 5:13

Speaking to yourselves in psalms and hymns and spiritual songs, singing and making melody in your heart to the Lord.

EPHESIANS 5:19

Kindness

And refused to obey, neither were mindful of thy wonders that thou didst among them; but hardened their necks, and in their rebellion appointed a captain to return to their bondage: but thou art a God ready to pardon, gracious and merciful, slow to anger, and of great kindness, and forsookest them not.

NEHEMIAH 9:17

But love ye your enemies, and do good, and lend, hoping for nothing again; and your reward shall be great, and ye shall be the children of the Highest: for he is kind unto the unthankful and to the evil.

LUKE 6:35

Charity suffereth long, and is kind; charity envieth not; charity vaunteth not itself, is not puffed up. . . beareth all things, believeth all things, hopeth all things, endureth all things. Charity never faileth.

1 CORINTHIANS 13:4, 7–8

But after that the kindness and love of God our Saviour toward man appeared, Not by works of righteousness which we have done, but according to his mercy he saved us, by the washing of regeneration, and renewing of the Holy Ghost.

TITUS 3:4–5

Who can find a virtuous woman? for her price is far above rubies. . . . She openeth her mouth with wisdom; and in her tongue is the law of kindness. . . . Favor is deceitful, and beauty is vain: but a woman that feareth the LORD, she shall be praised.

PROVERBS 31:10, 26, 30

In a little wrath I hid my face from thee for a moment; but with everlasting kindness will I have mercy on thee, saith the LORD thy Redeemer. . . . For the mountains shall depart, and the hills be removed; but my kindness shall not depart from thee.

ISAIAH 54:8, 10

And to godliness brotherly kindness; and to brotherly kindness charity. For if these things be in you, and abound. . .ye shall neither be barren nor unfruitful in the knowledge of our Lord Jesus Christ.

2 PETER 1:7–8

But in all things approving ourselves as the ministers of God. . .By pureness, by knowledge, by longsuffering, by kindness, by the Holy Ghost, by love unfeigned. . .as having nothing, and yet possessing all things.

2 CORINTHIANS 6:4, 6, 10

The desire of a man is his kindness: and a poor man is better than a liar. The fear of the LORD tendeth to life: and he that hath it shall abide satisfied.

PROVERBS 19:22–23

O praise the LORD, all ye nations: praise him, all ye people. For his merciful kindness is great toward us: and the truth of the LORD endureth for ever. Praise ye the LORD.

PSALM 117:1–2

Put on therefore, as the elect of God, holy and beloved, bowels of mercies, kindness, humbleness of mind, meekness, longsuffering. . .even as Christ forgave you, so also do ye.

COLOSSIANS 3:12–13

And he said, Blessed be thou of the LORD, my daughter: for thou hast shewed more kindness in the latter end than at the beginning. . . . And now, my daughter, fear not; I will do to thee all that thou requirest.

RUTH 3:10–11

Knowledge

⊹⊱⊰⊹

Now thanks be unto God, which always causeth us to triumph in Christ, and maketh manifest the savour of his knowledge by us in every place.

2 Corinthians 2:14

And I gave my heart to know wisdom, and to know madness and folly: I perceived that this also is vexation of spirit. For in much wisdom is much grief: and he that increaseth knowledge increaseth sorrow.

Ecclesiastes 1:17–18

O Lord, thou hast searched me, and known me. Thou knowest my downsitting and mine uprising, thou understandest my thought afar off. . . . Such knowledge is too wonderful for me; it is high, I cannot attain unto it.

Psalm 139:1–2, 6

That he would grant you, according to the riches of his glory, to be strengthened with might by his Spirit in the inner man. . .that ye, being rooted and grounded in love, May be able to comprehend. . .and to know the love of Christ, which passeth knowledge, that ye might be filled with all the fulness of God.

EPHESIANS 3:16–19

For to one is given by the Spirit the word of wisdom; to another the word of knowledge by the same Spirit. . .but all these worketh that one and the selfsame Spirit, dividing to every man severally as he will.

1 CORINTHIANS 12:8, 11

The heavens declare the glory of God. . . . Day unto day uttereth speech, and night unto night sheweth knowledge.

PSALM 19:1–2

All the words of my mouth are in righteousness. . . . They are all plain to him that understandeth, and right to them that find knowledge.

PROVERBS 8:8–9

Hearken unto this, O Job: stand still, and consider the wondrous works of God. . . . Dost thou know the balancings of the clouds, the wondrous works of him which is perfect in knowledge?

JOB 37:14, 16

Now when they saw the boldness of Peter and John, and perceived that they were unlearned and ignorant men, they marvelled; and they took knowledge of them, that they had been with Jesus.

ACTS 4:13

My people are destroyed for lack of knowledge: because thou hast rejected knowledge, I will also reject thee, that thou shalt be no priest to me: seeing thou hast forgotten the law of thy God.

HOSEA 4:6

And thou, child, shalt be called the prophet of the Highest: for thou shalt go before the face of the Lord to prepare his ways; To give knowledge of salvation unto his people by the remission of their sins.

LUKE 1:76–77

Forasmuch as an excellent spirit, and knowledge, and understanding, interpreting of dreams, and shewing of hard sentences, and dissolving of doubts, were found in the same Daniel. . .now let Daniel be called, and he will shew the interpretation.

DANIEL 5:12

My son, if thou wilt receive my words. . .yea, if thou criest after knowledge, and liftest up thy voice for understanding. . .then shalt thou understand the fear of the LORD, and find the knowledge of God. For the LORD giveth wisdom: out of his mouth cometh knowledge and understanding.

PROVERBS 2:1, 3, 5–6

And though I have the gift of prophecy, and understand all mysteries, and all knowledge: and though I have all faith, so that I could remove mountains, and have not charity, I am nothing.

1 CORINTHIANS 13:2

Labor

Whatsoever thy hand findeth to do, do it with thy might; for there is no work, nor device, nor knowledge, nor wisdom, in the grave, whither thou goest.

ECCLESIASTES 9:10

For even when we were with you, this we commanded you, that if any would not work, neither should he eat.

2 THESSALONIANS 3:10

And that ye study to be quiet, and to do your own business, and to work with your own hands, as we commanded you; that ye may walk honestly toward them that are without, and that ye may have lack of nothing.

1 THESSALONIANS 4:11–12

But if any provide not for his own, and specially for those of his own house, he hath denied the faith, and is worse than an infidel.

1 TIMOTHY 5:8

He becometh poor that dealeth with a slack hand: but the hand of the diligent maketh rich.

PROVERBS 10:4

The soul of the sluggard desireth, and hath nothing: but the soul of the diligent shall be made fat.

PROVERBS 13:4

Let him that stole steal no more: but rather let him labour, working with his hands the thing which is good, that he may have to give to him that needeth.

EPHESIANS 4:28

He that tilleth his land shall be satisfied with bread: but he that followeth vain persons is void of understanding.

PROVERBS 12:11

Not slothful in business; fervent in spirit; serving the Lord.

ROMANS 12:11

I know that there is no good in them, but for a man to rejoice, and to do good in his life. And also that every man should eat and drink, and enjoy the good of all his labour, it is the gift of God.

ECCLESIASTES 3:12–13

Love not sleep, lest thou come to poverty; open thine eyes, and thou shalt be satisfied with bread.

PROVERBS 20:13

The spider taketh hold with her hands, and is in kings' palaces.

PROVERBS 30:28

The hand of the diligent shall bear rule: but the slothful shall be under tribute.

PROVERBS 12:24

Wealth gotten by vanity shall be diminished: but he that gathereth by labour shall increase.

PROVERBS 13:11

For thou shalt eat the labour of thine hands: happy shalt thou be, and it shall be well with thee.

PSALM 128:2

Love of God

But as it is written, Eye hath not seen, nor ear heard, neither have entered into the heart of man, the things which God hath prepared for them that love him.

1 CORINTHIANS 2:9

Because he hath set his love upon me, therefore will I deliver him: I will set him on high, because he hath known my name. He shall call upon me, and I will answer him: I will be with him in trouble; I will deliver him, and honour him. With long life will I satisfy him, and shew him my salvation.

PSALM 91:14–16

I love them that love me; and those that seek me early shall find me.

PROVERBS 8:17

Know therefore that the LORD thy God, he is God, the faithful God, which keepeth covenant and mercy with them that love him and keep his commandments to a thousand generations.

DEUTERONOMY 7:9

Grace be with all them that love our Lord Jesus Christ in sincerity. Amen.

EPHESIANS 6:24

Trust in the LORD, and do good; so shalt thou dwell in the land, and verily thou shalt be fed. Delight thyself also in the LORD; and he shall give thee the desires of thine heart.

PSALM 37:3–4

The LORD preserveth all them that love him: but all the wicked will he destroy.

PSALM 145:20

And it shall come to pass, if ye shall hearken diligently unto my commandments which I command you this day, to love the LORD your God, and to serve him with all your heart and with all your soul, That I will give you the rain of your land in his due season, the first rain and the latter rain, that thou mayest gather in thy corn, and thy wine, and thine oil. And I will send grass in thy fields for thy cattle, that thou mayest eat and be full. Take heed to yourselves, that your heart be not deceived, and ye turn aside, and serve other gods, and worship them.

DEUTERONOMY 11:13–16

He that hath my commandments, and keepeth them, he it is that loveth me: and he that loveth me shall be loved of my Father, and I will love him, and will manifest myself to him.

JOHN 14:21

Love of Others

Seeing ye have purified your souls in obeying the truth through the Spirit unto unfeigned love of the brethren, see that ye love one another with a pure heart fervently.

1 PETER 1:22

And above all these things put on charity, which is the bond of perfectness.

COLOSSIANS 3:14

But as touching brotherly love ye need not that I write unto you: for ye yourselves are taught of God to love one another. And indeed ye do it toward all the brethren which are in all Macedonia: but we beseech you, brethren, that ye increase more and more.

1 THESSALONIANS 4:9–10

A new commandment I give unto you, That ye love one another; as I have loved you, that ye also love one another. By this shall all men know that ye are my disciples, if ye have love one to another.

JOHN 13:34–35

Beloved, let us love one another: for love is of God; and every one that loveth is born of God, and knoweth God. He that loveth not knoweth not God; for God is love. In this was manifested the love of God toward us, because that God sent his only begotten Son into the world, that we might live through him. Herein is love, not that we loved God, but that he loved us, and sent his Son to be the propitiation for our sins. Beloved, if God so loved us, we ought also to love one another.

1 JOHN 4:7–11

He that loveth his brother abideth in the light, and there is none occasion of stumbling in him. But he that hateth his brother is in darkness, and walketh in darkness, and knoweth not whither he goeth, because that darkness hath blinded his eyes.

1 JOHN 2:10–11

Mercy

But love ye your enemies, and do good, and lend, hoping for nothing again. . . . Be ye therefore merciful, as your Father also is merciful.

LUKE 6:35–36

Therefore hath the LORD recompensed me according to my righteousness, according to the cleanness of my hands in his eyesight. With the merciful thou wilt shew thyself merciful; with an upright man thou wilt shew thyself upright. . . . For thou wilt save the afflicted people.

PSALM 18:24–25, 27

And the LORD passed by before him, and proclaimed, The LORD, The LORD God, merciful and gracious, longsuffering, and abundant in goodness and truth, Keeping mercy for thousands, forgiving iniquity and transgression and sin.

EXODUS 34:6–7

For if ye turn again unto the Lord, your brethren and your children shall find compassion before them that lead them captive, so that they shall come again into this land: for the Lord your God is gracious and merciful, and will not turn away his face from you, if ye return unto him.

2 Chronicles 30:9

And therefore will the Lord wait, that he may be gracious unto you, and therefore will he be exalted, that he may have mercy upon you: for the Lord is a God of judgment: blessed are all they that wait for him.

Isaiah 30:18

And they shall not teach every man his neighbour, and every man his brother, saying, Know the Lord: for all shall know me, from the least to the greatest. For I will be merciful to their unrighteousness, and their sins and their iniquities will I remember no more.

Hebrews 8:11–12

Wherefore in all things it behoved him to be made like unto his brethren, that he might be a merciful and faithful high priest in things pertaining to God, to make reconciliation for the sins of the people. For in that he himself hath suffered being tempted, he is able to succour them that are tempted.

HEBREWS 2:17–18

It is good that a man should both hope and quietly wait for the salvation of the LORD. . . . For the Lord will not cast off for ever: But though he cause grief, yet will he have compassion according to the multitude of his mercies.

LAMENTATIONS 3:26, 31–32

It is of the LORD's mercies that we are not consumed, because his compassions fail not. They are new every morning: great is thy faithfulness.

LAMENTATIONS 3:22–23

Blessed are the merciful: for they shall obtain mercy.

MATTHEW 5:7

But they and our fathers dealt proudly, and hardened their necks, and hearkened not to thy commandments, And refused to obey. . .and in their rebellion appointed a captain to return to their bondage: but thou art a God ready to pardon, gracious and merciful, slow to anger, and of great kindness, and forsookest them not.

NEHEMIAH 9:16–17

Therefore also now, saith the LORD, turn ye even to me with all your heart, and with fasting, and with weeping, and with mourning: And rend your heart, and not your garments, and turn unto the LORD your God: for he is gracious and merciful, slow to anger, and of great kindness, and repenteth him of the evil. Who knoweth if he will return and repent, and leave a blessing behind him?

JOEL 2:12–14

The merciful man doeth good to his own soul: but he that is cruel troubleth his own flesh.

PROVERBS 11:17

Modesty

In like manner also, that women adorn themselves in modest apparel, with shamefacedness and sobriety; not with broided hair, or gold, or pearls, or costly array; But (which becometh women professing godliness) with good works.

1 Timothy 2:9–10

For I am jealous over you with godly jealousy: for I have espoused you to one husband, that I may present you as a chaste virgin to Christ. But I fear, lest by any means, as the serpent beguiled Eve through his subtilty, so your minds should be corrupted from the simplicity that is in Christ.

2 Corinthians 11:2–3

Be not deceived: evil communications corrupt good manners. Awake to righteousness, and sin not.

1 Corinthians 15:33–34

Likewise, ye wives, be in subjection to your own husbands; that, if any obey not the word, they also may without the word be won by the conversation of the wives; While they behold your chaste conversation coupled with fear.

1 Peter 3:1–2

The aged women likewise, that they be in behaviour as becometh holiness, not false accusers, not given to much wine, teachers of good things; That they may teach the young women to be sober, to love their husbands, to love their children, To be discreet, chaste, keepers at home, good, obedient to their own husbands, that the word of God be not blasphemed.

Titus 2:3–5

As a jewel of gold in a swine's snout, so is a fair woman which is without discretion.

Proverbs 11:22

Motherhood

Then one said unto him, Behold, thy mother and thy brethren stand without, desiring to speak with thee. But he answered and said unto him. . .Who is my mother? and who are my brethren? And he stretched forth his hand toward his disciples, and said, Behold my mother and my brethren! For whosoever shall do the will of my Father which is in heaven, the same is my brother, and sister, and mother.

MATTHEW 12:47–50

Then sang Deborah and Barak the son of Abinoam on that day, saying, Praise ye the LORD for the avenging of Israel, when the people willingly offered themselves. . . . The inhabitants of the villages ceased, they ceased in Israel, until that I Deborah arose, that I arose a mother in Israel.

JUDGES 5:1–2, 7

And Adam called his wife's name Eve; because she was the mother of all living.

GENESIS 3:20

Howbeit in vain do they worship me, teaching for doctrines the commandments of men. . . . For Moses said, Honour thy father and thy mother; and, Whoso curseth father or mother, let him die the death: But ye say, If a man shall say to his father or mother, It is Corban, that is to say, a gift, by whatsoever thou mightest be profited by me; he shall be free. And ye suffer him no more to do ought for his father or his mother; Making the word of God of none effect through your tradition, which ye have delivered: and many such like things do ye.

MARK 7:7, 10–13

He maketh the barren woman to keep house, and to be a joyful mother of children. Praise ye the LORD.

PSALM 113:9

My son, keep thy father's commandment, and forsake not the law of thy mother: Bind them continually upon thine heart, and tie them about thy neck. When thou goest, it shall lead thee; when thou sleepest, it shall keep thee; and when thou awakest, it shall talk with thee. For the commandment is a lamp; and the law is light; and reproofs of instruction are the way of life.

PROVERBS 6:20–23

Hearken unto thy father that begat thee, and despise not thy mother when she is old.

PROVERBS 23:22

Obedience

Now therefore, if ye will obey my voice indeed, and keep my covenant, then ye shall be a peculiar treasure unto me above all people: for all the earth is mine.

EXODUS 19:5

Thou shalt keep therefore his statutes, and his commandments, which I command thee this day, that it may go well with thee, and with thy children after thee, and that thou mayest prolong thy days upon the earth, which the LORD thy God giveth thee, for ever.

DEUTERONOMY 4:40

But whoso looketh into the perfect law of liberty, and continueth therein, he being not a forgetful hearer, but a doer of the work, this man shall be blessed in his deed.

JAMES 1:25

Observe and hear all these words which I command thee, that it may go well with thee, and with thy children after thee for ever, when thou doest that which is good and right in the sight of the LORD thy God.

DEUTERONOMY 12:28

My son, forget not my law; but let thine heart keep my commandments: For length of days, and long life, and peace, shall they add to thee.

PROVERBS 3:1–2

Those things, which ye have both learned, and received, and heard, and seen in me, do: and the God of peace shall be with you.

PHILIPPIANS 4:9

If they obey and serve him, they shall spend their days in prosperity, and their years in pleasures.

JOB 36:11

I command thee this day to love the LORD thy God, to walk in his ways, and to keep his commandments and his statutes and his judgments, that thou mayest live and multiply: and the LORD thy God shall bless thee in the land whither thou goest to possess it.

DEUTERONOMY 30:16

Not every one that saith unto me, Lord, Lord, shall enter into the kingdom of heaven; but he that doeth the will of my Father which is in heaven.

MATTHEW 7:21

Let us hear the conclusion of the whole matter: Fear God, and keep his commandments: for this is the whole duty of man.

ECCLESIASTES 12:13

Blessed are they that keep his testimonies, and that seek him with the whole heart.

PSALM 119:2

If ye keep my commandments, ye shall abide in my love; even as I have kept my Father's commandments, and abide in his love.

John 15:10

All the paths of the LORD are mercy and truth unto such as keep his covenant and his testimonies.

Psalm 25:10

For not the hearers of the law are just before God, but the doers of the law shall be justified.

Romans 2:13

And Samuel said, Hath the LORD as great delight in burnt offerings and sacrifices, as in obeying the voice of the LORD? Behold, to obey is better than sacrifice, and to hearken than the fat of rams.

1 Samuel 15:22

Whosoever therefore shall break one of these least commandments, and shall teach men so, he shall be called the least in the kingdom of heaven: but whosoever shall do and teach them, the same shall be called great in the kingdom of heaven.

MATTHEW 5:19

And the world passeth away, and the lust thereof: but he that doeth the will of God abideth for ever.

1 JOHN 2:17

Furthermore we have had fathers of our flesh which corrected us, and we gave them reverence: shall we not much rather be in subjection unto the Father of spirits, and live?

HEBREWS 12:9

Wherefore, my beloved, as ye have always obeyed, not as in my presence only, but now much more in my absence, work out your own salvation with fear and trembling.

PHILIPPIANS 2:12

If ye be willing and obedient, ye shall eat the good of the land.

ISAIAH 1:19

But he said, Yea rather, blessed are they that hear the word of God, and keep it.

LUKE 11:28

Keep therefore the words of this covenant, and do them, that ye may prosper in all that ye do.

DEUTERONOMY 29:9

Patience

I waited patiently for the LORD; and he inclined unto me, and heard my cry. He brought me up also out of an horrible pit, out of the miry clay, and set my feet upon a rock, and established my goings. And he hath put a new song in my mouth, even praise unto our God: many shall see it, and fear, and shall trust in the LORD.

PSALM 40:1–3

Cast not away therefore your confidence, which hath great recompence of reward. For ye have need of patience, that, after ye have done the will of God, ye might receive the promise.

HEBREWS 10:35–36

A bishop then must be blameless. . .Not given to wine, no striker, not greedy of filthy lucre; but patient, not a brawler, not covetous.

1 TIMOTHY 3:2–3

Be patient therefore, brethren, unto the coming of the Lord. Behold, the husbandman waiteth for the precious fruit of the earth, and hath long patience for it, until he receive the early and latter rain. Be ye also patient; stablish your hearts: for the coming of the Lord draweth nigh.

JAMES 5:7–8

And we desire that every one of you do shew the same diligence to the full assurance of hope unto the end: That ye be not slothful, but followers of them who through faith and patience inherit the promises.

HEBREWS 6:11–12

Because thou hast kept the word of my patience, I also will keep thee from the hour of temptation, which shall come upon all the world, to try them that dwell upon the earth.

REVELATION 3:10

And not only so, but we glory in tribulations also: knowing that tribulation worketh patience; And patience experience; and experience, hope: And hope maketh not ashamed; because the love of God is shed abroad in our hearts by the Holy Ghost which is given unto us.

Romans 5:3–5

Wherefore seeing we also are compassed about with so great a cloud of witnesses, let us lay aside every weight, and the sin which doth so easily beset us, and let us run with patience the race that is set before us.

Hebrews 12:1

Better is the end of a thing than the beginning thereof: and the patient in spirit is better than the proud in spirit.

Ecclesiastes 7:8

For whatsoever things were written aforetime were written for our learning, that we through patience and comfort of the scriptures might have hope. Now the God of patience and consolation grant you to be likeminded one toward another according to Christ Jesus.

ROMANS 15:4–5

Rest in the LORD, and wait patiently for him: fret not thyself because of him who prospereth in his way, because of the man who bringeth wicked devices to pass.

PSALM 37:7

And the servant of the Lord must not strive; but be gentle unto all men, apt to teach, patient.

2 TIMOTHY 2:24

Peace

For the mountains shall depart, and the hills be removed; but my kindness shall not depart from thee, neither shall the covenant of my peace be removed, saith the Lord that hath mercy on thee. . . . And all thy children shall be taught of the Lord; and great shall be the peace of thy children.

Isaiah 54:10, 13

Thou wilt keep him in perfect peace, whose mind is stayed on thee: because he trusteth in thee. Trust ye in the Lord for ever: for in the Lord Jehovah is everlasting strength.

Isaiah 26:3–4

These things I have spoken unto you, that in me ye might have peace. In the world ye shall have tribulation: but be of good cheer; I have overcome the world.

John 16:33

For he that will love life, and see good days, let him refrain his tongue from evil, and his lips that they speak no guile: Let him eschew evil, and do good; let him seek peace, and ensue it.

1 Peter 3:10–11

Peace I leave with you, my peace I give unto you: not as the world giveth, give I unto you. Let not your heart be troubled, neither let it be afraid.

John 14:27

Mark the perfect man, and behold the upright: for the end of that man is peace. . . . But the salvation of the righteous is of the Lord: he is their strength in the time of trouble. And the Lord shall help them, and deliver them: he shall deliver them from the wicked, and save them, because they trust in him.

Psalm 37:37, 39–40

Now the God of hope fill you with all joy and peace in believing, that ye may abound in hope, through the power of the Holy Ghost.

ROMANS 15:13

And the very God of peace sanctify you wholly; and I pray God your whole spirit and soul and body be preserved blameless unto the coming of our Lord Jesus Christ.

1 THESSALONIANS 5:23

For ye shall go out with joy, and be led forth with peace: the mountains and the hills shall break forth before you into singing, and all the trees of the field shall clap their hands. Instead of the thorn shall come up the fir tree, and instead of the brier shall come up the myrtle tree: and it shall be to the LORD for a name, for an everlasting sign that shall not be cut off.

ISAIAH 55:12–13

These things, which ye have both learned, and received, and heard, and seen in me, do: and the God of peace shall be with you.

PHILIPPIANS 4:9

Great peace have they which love thy law: and nothing shall offend them.

PSALM 119:165

And the fruit of righteousness is sown in peace of them that make peace.

JAMES 3:18

When a man's ways please the LORD, he maketh even his enemies to be at peace with him.

PROVERBS 16:7

Persistence

Then said Jesus to those Jews which believed on him, If ye continue in my word, then are ye my disciples indeed; And ye shall know the truth, and the truth shall make you free.

JOHN 8:31–32

The LORD will give strength unto his people; the LORD will bless his people with peace.

PSALM 29:11

Stand therefore, having your loins girt about with truth, and having on the breastplate of righteousness; And your feet shod with the preparation of the gospel of peace; Above all, taking the shield of faith, wherewith ye shall be able to quench all the fiery darts of the wicked. And take the helmet of salvation, and the sword of the Spirit, which is the word of God.

EPHESIANS 6:14–17

For I am in a strait betwixt two, having a desire to depart, and to be with Christ; which is far better: Nevertheless to abide in the flesh is more needful for you. And having this confidence, I know that I shall abide and continue with you all for your furtherance and joy of faith.

PHILIPPIANS 1:23–25

If ye continue in the faith grounded and settled, and be not moved away from the hope of the gospel, which ye have heard, and which was preached to every creature which is under heaven. . .whereunto I also labour, striving according to his working, which worketh in me mightily.

COLOSSIANS 1:23, 29

My mercy will I keep for him for evermore, and my covenant shall stand fast with him. His seed also will I make to endure for ever, and his throne as the days of heaven.

PSALM 89:28–29

Out of the depths have I cried unto thee, O Lord. Lord, hear my voice: let thine ears be attentive to the voice of my supplications. If thou, Lord, shouldest mark iniquities, O Lord, who shall stand? But there is forgiveness with thee, that thou mayest be feared. I wait for the Lord, my soul doth wait, and in his word do I hope.

Psalm 130:1–5

And they truly were many priests, because they were not suffered to continue by reason of death: But this man, because he continueth ever, hath an unchangeable priesthood.

Hebrews 7:23–24

Thus saith the Lord, Stand ye in the ways, and see, and ask for the old paths, where is the good way, and walk therein, and ye shall find rest for your souls.

Jeremiah 6:16

There are many devices in a man's heart; nevertheless the counsel of the LORD, that shall stand.

PROVERBS 19:21

The grass withereth, the flower fadeth: but the word of our God shall stand for ever.

ISAIAH 40:8

And I beheld when he had opened the sixth seal, and, lo, there was a great earthquake; and the sun became black as sackcloth of hair, and the moon became as blood. . . . And the kings of the earth, and the great men, and the rich men, and the chief captains, and the mighty men, and every bondman, and every free man, hid themselves in the dens and in the rocks of the mountains. . .for the great day of his wrath is come; and who shall be able to stand?

REVELATION 6:12, 15, 17

O continue thy lovingkindness unto them that know thee; and thy righteousness to the upright in heart.

PSALM 36:10

Prayer

And this is the confidence that we have in him, that, if we ask any thing according to his will, he heareth us: And if we know that he hear us, whatsoever we ask, we know that we have the petitions that we desired of him.

1 John 5:14–15

Now mine eyes shall be open, and mine ears attent unto the prayer that is made in this place. For now have I chosen and sanctified this house, that my name may be there for ever: and mine eyes and mine heart shall be there perpetually.

2 Chronicles 7:15–16

And Jesus went into the temple of God, and cast out all them that sold and bought in the temple, and overthrew the tables of the moneychangers, and the seats of them that sold doves, And said unto them, It is written, My house shall be called the house of prayer; but ye have made it a den of thieves.

Matthew 21:12–13

And whatsoever ye shall ask in my name, that will I do, that the Father may be glorified in the Son. If ye shall ask any thing in my name, I will do it.

John 14:13–14

I beseech thee, O Lord God of heaven, the great and terrible God, that keepeth covenant and mercy for them that love him and observe his commandments: Let thine ear now be attentive, and thine eyes open, that thou mayest hear the prayer of thy servant, which I pray before thee now, day and night, for the children of Israel thy servants.

Nehemiah 1:5–6

And in that day ye shall ask me nothing. Verily, verily, I say unto you, Whatsoever ye shall ask the Father in my name, he will give it you. Hitherto have ye asked nothing in my name: ask, and ye shall receive, that your joy may be full.

John 16:23–24

Then shall ye call upon me, and ye shall go and pray unto me, and I will hearken unto you. And ye shall seek me, and find me, when ye shall search for me with all your heart.

JEREMIAH 29:12–13

And he spake a parable unto them to this end, that men ought always to pray, and not to faint.

LUKE 18:1

Praise waiteth for thee, O God, in Sion: and unto thee shall the vow be performed. O thou that hearest prayer, unto thee shall all flesh come.

PSALM 65:1–2

Be careful for nothing; but in every thing by prayer and supplication with thanksgiving let your requests be made known unto God. And the peace of God, which passeth all understanding, shall keep your hearts and minds through Christ Jesus.

PHILIPPIANS 4:6–7

But thou, when thou prayest, enter into thy closet, and when thou hast shut thy door, pray to thy Father which is in secret; and thy Father which seeth in secret shall reward thee openly. But when ye pray, use not vain repetitions, as the heathen do: for they think that they shall be heard for their much speaking. Be not ye therefore like unto them: for your Father knoweth what things ye have need of, before ye ask him. After this manner therefore pray ye: Our Father which art in heaven, Hallowed be thy name. Thy kingdom come. Thy will be done in earth, as it is in heaven.

MATTHEW 6:6–10

For verily I say unto you, That whosoever shall say unto this mountain, Be thou removed, and be thou cast into the sea; and shall not doubt in his heart, but shall believe that those things which he saith shall come to pass; he shall have whatsoever he saith. Therefore I say unto you, What things soever ye desire, when ye pray, believe that ye receive them, and ye shall have them.

MARK 11:23–24

Is any among you afflicted? let him pray. Is any merry? let him sing psalms. Is any sick among you? let him call for the elders of the church; and let them pray over him, anointing him with oil in the name of the Lord: And the prayer of faith shall save the sick, and the Lord shall raise him up; and if he have committed sins, they shall be forgiven him.

JAMES 5:13–15

Thou shalt make thy prayer unto him, and he shall hear thee, and thou shalt pay thy vows. Thou shalt also decree a thing, and it shall be established unto thee: and the light shall shine upon thy ways.

JOB 22:27–28

The effectual fervent prayer of a righteous man availeth much. Elias was a man subject to like passions as we are, and he prayed earnestly that it might not rain: and it rained not on the earth by the space of three years and six months. And he prayed again, and the heaven gave rain, and the earth brought forth her fruit.

JAMES 5:16–18

Preparation

If a man therefore purge himself from these, he shall be a vessel unto honour, sanctified, and meet for the master's use, and prepared unto every good work.

2 TIMOTHY 2:21

In my Father's house are many mansions: if it were not so, I would have told you. I go to prepare a place for you. And if I go and prepare a place for you, I will come again, and receive you unto myself; that where I am, there ye may be also.

JOHN 14:2–3

By faith Noah, being warned of God of things not seen as yet, moved with fear, prepared an ark to the saving of his house: by the which he condemned the world, and became heir of the righteousness which is by faith.

HEBREWS 11:7

And I saw a new heaven and a new earth: for the first heaven and the first earth were passed away; and there was no more sea. And I John saw the holy city, new Jerusalem, coming down from God out of heaven, prepared as a bride adorned for her husband.

REVELATION 21:1–2

Thou, O God, didst send a plentiful rain, whereby thou didst confirm thine inheritance, when it was weary. Thy congregation hath dwelt therein: thou, O God, hast prepared of thy goodness for the poor.

PSALM 68:9–10

Wherefore when he cometh into the world, he saith, Sacrifice and offering thou wouldest not, but a body hast thou prepared me.

HEBREWS 10:5

Thou preparest a table before me in the presence of mine enemies: thou anointest my head with oil; my cup runneth over.

PSALM 23:5

And David made him houses in the city of David, and prepared a place for the ark of God, and pitched for it a tent.

1 CHRONICLES 15:1

And he saith unto them, Ye shall drink indeed of my cup, and be baptized with the baptism that I am baptized with; but to sit on my right hand, and on my left, is not mine to give, but it shall be given to them for whom it is prepared of my Father.

MATTHEW 20:23

Protection

The eternal God is thy refuge, and underneath are the everlasting arms.

DEUTERONOMY 33:27

The LORD also will be a refuge for the oppressed, a refuge in times of trouble.

PSALM 9:9

God is our refuge and strength, a very present help in trouble.

PSALM 46:1

When thou passest through the waters, I will be with thee; and through the rivers, they shall not overflow thee: when thou walkest through the fire, thou shalt not be burned; neither shall the flame kindle upon thee.

ISAIAH 43:2

But the LORD is my defence; and my God is the rock of my refuge.

PSALM 94:22

In the fear of the LORD is strong confidence: and his children shall have a place of refuge.

PROVERBS 14:26

Be thou my strong habitation, whereunto I may continually resort: thou hast given commandment to save me; for thou art my rock and my fortress.

PSALM 71:3

Above all, taking the shield of faith, wherewith ye shall be able to quench all the fiery darts of the wicked.

EPHESIANS 6:16

For thou, LORD, wilt bless the righteous; with favour wilt thou compass him as with a shield.

PSALM 5:12

The LORD liveth; and blessed be my rock; and exalted be the God of the rock of my salvation.

2 SAMUEL 22:47

Thou hast also given me the shield of thy salvation: and thy right hand hath holden me up, and thy gentleness hath made me great.

PSALM 18:35

The LORD is my rock, and my fortress, and my deliverer; my God, my strength, in whom I will trust; my buckler, and the horn of my salvation, and my high tower.

PSALM 18:2

The name of the LORD is a strong tower: the righteous runneth into it, and is safe.

PROVERBS 18:10

Our soul waiteth for the LORD: he is our help and our shield.

PSALM 33:20

Every word of God is pure: he is a shield unto them that put their trust in him.

PROVERBS 30:5

He shall cover thee with his feathers, and under his wings shalt thou trust: his truth shall be thy shield and buckler.

PSALM 91:4

But whoso hearkeneth unto me shall dwell safely, and shall be quiet from fear of evil.

PROVERBS 1:33

And he said, The LORD is my rock, and my fortress, and my deliverer; the God of my rock; in him will I trust: he is my shield, and the horn of my salvation, my high tower, and my refuge, my saviour; thou savest me from violence. I will call on the LORD, who is worthy to be praised: so shall I be saved from mine enemies.

2 SAMUEL 22:2–4

The Lord is good, a strong hold in the day of trouble;
and he knoweth them that trust in him.

NAHUM 1:7

Cast thy burden upon the Lord, and he shall sustain
thee: he shall never suffer the righteous to be moved.

PSALM 55:22

For thou art my rock and my fortress; therefore for
thy name's sake lead me, and guide me.

PSALM 31:3

God is our refuge and strength, a very present help in
trouble. Therefore will not we fear, though the earth
be removed, and though the mountains be carried
into the midst of the sea; though the waters thereof
roar and be troubled, Though the mountains shake
with the swelling thereof. Selah.

PSALM 46:1–3

Purity

Let us draw near with a true heart in full assurance of faith, having our hearts sprinkled from an evil conscience, and our bodies washed with pure water.

HEBREWS 10:22

The thoughts of the wicked are an abomination to the LORD: but the words of the pure are pleasant words.

PROVERBS 15:26

With the pure thou wilt shew thyself pure; and with the froward thou wilt shew thyself unsavoury. And the afflicted people thou wilt save: but thine eyes are upon the haughty, that thou mayest bring them down.

2 SAMUEL 22:27–28

Let us therefore follow after the things which make for peace, and things wherewith one may edify another. For meat destroy not the work of God. All things indeed are pure; but it is evil for that man who eateth with offence.

ROMANS 14:19–20

This second epistle, beloved, I now write unto you; in both which I stir up your pure minds by way of remembrance: That ye may be mindful of the words which were spoken before by the holy prophets, and of the commandment of us the apostles of the Lord and Saviour.

2 PETER 3:1–2

Art thou not from everlasting, O LORD my God, mine Holy One? . . . Thou art of purer eyes than to behold evil, and canst not look on iniquity.

HABAKKUK 1:12–13

Pure religion and undefiled before God and the Father is this, To visit the fatherless and widows in their affliction, and to keep himself unspotted from the world.

James 1:27

Finally, brethren, whatsoever things are true, whatsoever things are honest, whatsoever things are just, whatsoever things are pure, whatsoever things are lovely, whatsoever things are of good report; if there be any virtue, and if there be any praise, think on these things.

Philippians 4:8

The words of the Lord are pure words: as silver tried in a furnace of earth, purified seven times. Thou shalt keep them, O Lord, thou shalt preserve them from this generation for ever.

Psalm 12:6–7

Even a child is known by his doings, whether his work be pure, and whether it be right.

PROVERBS 20:11

Unto the pure all things are pure: but unto them that are defiled and unbelieving is nothing pure; but even their mind and conscience is defiled.

TITUS 1:15

Every word of God is pure: he is a shield unto them that put their trust in him. Add thou not unto his words, lest he reprove thee, and thou be found a liar.

PROVERBS 30:5–6

Blessed are the pure in heart: for they shall see God.

MATTHEW 5:8

Repentance

For it is impossible for those who were once enlightened, and have tasted of the heavenly gift, and were made partakers of the Holy Ghost, And have tasted the good word of God, and the powers of the world to come, If they shall fall away, to renew them again unto repentance; seeing they crucify to themselves the Son of God afresh, and put him to an open shame.

HEBREWS 6:4–6

For I would not, brethren, that ye should be ignorant of this mystery, lest ye should be wise in your own conceits; that blindness in part is happened to Israel, until the fullness of the Gentiles be come in. . . . For this is my covenant unto them, when I shall take away their sins. . . . For the gifts and calling of God are without repentance.

ROMANS 11:25, 27, 29

The LORD is nigh unto them that are of a broken heart; and saveth such as be of a contrite spirit. Many are the afflictions of the righteous: but the LORD delivereth him out of them all.

PSALM 34:18–19

Whereupon, O king Agrippa, I was not disobedient unto the heavenly vision: But shewed first unto them of Damascus, and at Jerusalem, and throughout all the coasts of Judaea, and then to the Gentiles, that they should repent and turn to God, and do works meet for repentance.

ACTS 26:19–20

For godly sorrow worketh repentance to salvation not to be repented of: but the sorrow of the world worketh death.

2 CORINTHIANS 7:10

In those days came John the Baptist, preaching in the wilderness of Judaea, And saying, Repent ye: for the kingdom of heaven is at hand. For this is he that was spoken of by the prophet Esaias, saying, The voice of one crying in the wilderness, Prepare ye the way of the Lord, make his paths straight.

MATTHEW 3:1–3

The Lord is not slack concerning his promise, as some men count slackness; but is longsuffering to us-ward, not willing that any should perish, but that all should come to repentance.

2 PETER 3:9

Righteousness

❦ ❦

My little children, these things write I unto you, that ye sin not. And if any man sin, we have an advocate with the Father, Jesus Christ the righteous: And he is the propitiation for our sins: and not for ours only, but also for the sins of the whole world.

1 JOHN 2:1–2

Righteous art thou, O LORD, and upright are thy judgments. Thy testimonies that thou hast commanded are righteous and very faithful. . . . Thy righteousness is an everlasting righteousness, and thy law is the truth. . . . The righteousness of thy testimonies is everlasting: give me understanding and I shall live.

PSALM 119:137–138, 142, 144

Treasures of wickedness profit nothing: but righteousness delivereth from death. The LORD will not suffer the soul of the righteous to famish: but he casteth away the substance of the wicked.

PROVERBS 10:2–3

The righteous is delivered out of trouble, and the wicked cometh in his stead. . . . Though hand join in hand, the wicked shall not be unpunished: but the seed of the righteous shall be delivered.

PROVERBS 11:8, 21

Therefore as by the offence of one judgment came upon all men to condemnation; even so by the righteousness of one the free gift came upon all men unto justification of life. For as by one man's disobedience many were made sinners, so by the obedience of one shall many be made righteous.

ROMANS 5:18–19

Whosoever abideth in him sinneth not: whosoever sinneth hath not seen him, neither known him. Little children, let no man deceive you: he that doeth righteousness is righteous, even as he is righteous.

1 John 3:6–7

For the time is come that judgment must begin at the house of God: and if it first begin at us, what shall the end be of them that obey not the gospel of God? And if the righteous scarcely be saved, where shall the ungodly and the sinner appear?

1 Peter 4:17–18

The lips of the righteous feed many: but fools die for want of wisdom. . . . The hope of the righteous shall be gladness: but the expectation of the wicked shall perish.

Proverbs 10:21, 28

Seeking

For thus saith the Lord unto the house of Israel, Seek ye me, and ye shall live: But seek not Bethel, nor enter into Gilgal, and pass not to Beersheba. . . . Seek the Lord, and ye shall live.

Amos 5:4–6

Doth not wisdom cry? and understanding put forth her voice? . . . I love them that love me; and those that seek me early shall find me.

Proverbs 8:1, 17

Of which salvation the prophets have enquired and searched diligently, who prophesied of the grace that should come unto you: Searching what, or what manner of time the Spirit of Christ which was in them did signify, when it testified beforehand the sufferings of Christ, and the glory that should follow.

1 Peter 1:10–11

Therefore take no thought, saying, What shall we eat? or, What shall we drink? or, Wherewithal shall we be clothed? . . . But seek ye first the kingdom of God, and his righteousness; and all these things shall be added unto you.

MATTHEW 6:31, 33

Ask, and it shall be given you; seek, and ye shall find; knock, and it shall be opened unto you: For every one that asketh receiveth; and he that seeketh findeth; and to him that knocketh it shall be opened.

MATTHEW 7:7–8

If ye then be risen with Christ, seek those things which are above, where Christ sitteth on the right hand of God. Set your affection on things above, not on things on the earth. For ye are dead, and your life is hid with Christ in God.

COLOSSIANS 3:1–3

Search me, O God, and know my heart: try me, and know my thoughts: And see if there be any wicked way in me, and lead me in the way everlasting.

PSALM 139:23–24

For I know the thoughts that I think toward you, saith the LORD, thoughts of peace, and not of evil, to give you an expected end.

JEREMIAH 29:11

Whosoever shall seek to save his life shall lose it; and whosoever shall lose his life shall preserve it.

LUKE 17:33

Service

And thou, Solomon my son, know thou the God of thy father, and serve him with a perfect heart and with a willing mind: for the LORD searcheth all hearts, and understandeth all the imaginations of the thoughts: if thou seek him, he will be found of thee; but if thou forsake him, he will cast thee off for ever.

1 CHRONICLES 28:9

And there was one Anna, a prophetess, the daughter of Phanuel, of the tribe of Aser. . . And she. . . departed not from the temple, but served God with fastings and prayers night and day.

LUKE 2:36–37

And Moses said unto God, Who am I, that I should go unto Pharaoh, and that I should bring forth the children of Israel out of Egypt? And he said, Certainly I will be with thee; and this shall be a token unto thee, that I have sent thee: When thou hast brought forth the people out of Egypt, ye shall serve God upon this mountain.

EXODUS 3:11–12

Make a joyful noise unto the LORD, all ye lands. Serve the LORD with gladness: come before his presence with singing.

PSALM 100:1–2

No servant can serve two masters: for either he will hate the one, and love the other; or else he will hold to the one, and despise the other. Ye cannot serve God and mammon.

LUKE 16:13

Then Jesus six days before the passover came to Bethany, where Lazarus was which had been dead, whom he raised from the dead. There they made him a supper; and Martha served.

JOHN 12:1–2

Then the king commanded, and they brought Daniel, and cast him into the den of lions. Now the king spake and said unto Daniel, Thy God whom thou servest continually, he will deliver thee.

DANIEL 6:16

Then saith Jesus unto him, Get thee hence, Satan: for it is written, Thou shalt worship the Lord thy God, and him only shalt thou serve.

MATTHEW 4:10

Sincerity

For our rejoicing is this, the testimony of our conscience, that in simplicity and godly sincerity, not with fleshly wisdom, but by the grace of God, we have had our conversation in the world, and more abundantly to you-ward.

2 Corinthians 1:12

Wherefore laying aside all malice, and all guile, and hypocrisies, and envies, and all evil speakings, As newborn babes, desire the sincere milk of the word, that ye may grow thereby: If so be ye have tasted that the Lord is gracious.

1 Peter 2:1–3

Peace be to the brethren, and love with faith, from God the Father and the Lord Jesus Christ. Grace be with all them that love our Lord Jesus Christ in sincerity. Amen.

EPHESIANS 6:23–24

For even Christ our passover is sacrificed for us: Therefore let us keep the feast, not with old leaven, neither with the leaven of malice and wickedness; but with the unleavened bread of sincerity and truth.

1 CORINTHIANS 5:7–8

And this I pray, that your love may abound yet more and more in knowledge and in all judgment; That ye may approve things that are excellent; that ye may be sincere and without offence till the day of Christ.

PHILIPPIANS 1:9–10

Strength

Therefore will I divide him a portion with the great, and he shall divide the spoil with the strong; because he hath poured out his soul unto death: and he was numbered with the transgressors; and he bare the sin of many, and made intercession for the transgressor.

ISAIAH 53:12

Their Redeemer is strong; the LORD of hosts is his name: he shall thoroughly plead their cause, that he may give rest to the land, and disquiet the inhabitants of Babylon.

JEREMIAH 50:34

And thou, child, shalt be called the prophet of the Highest: for thou shalt go before the face of the Lord to prepare his ways. . . . And the child grew, and waxed strong in spirit, and was in the deserts till the day of his shewing unto Israel.

LUKE 1:76, 80

And when they had performed all things according to the law of the Lord, they returned into Galilee, to their own city Nazareth. And the child grew, and waxed strong in spirit, filled with wisdom; and the grace of God was upon him.

LUKE 2:39–40

But to that also which is of the faith of Abraham; who is the father of us all. . . . And being not weak in faith, he considered not his own body now dead, when he was about an hundred years old, neither yet the deadness of Sara's womb: He staggered not at the promise of God through unbelief; but was strong in faith, giving glory to God.

ROMANS 4:16, 19–20

Be thou my strong habitation, whereunto I may continually resort: thou hast given commandment to save me; for thou art my rock and my fortress.

PSALM 71:3

And he said unto me, My grace is sufficient for thee: for my strength is made perfect in weakness. Most gladly therefore will I rather glory in my infirmities, that the power of Christ may rest upon me. Therefore I take pleasure in infirmities, in reproaches, in necessities, in persecutions, in distresses for Christ's sake: for when I am weak, then am I strong.

2 Corinthians 12:9–10

I can do all things through Christ which strengtheneth me.

Philippians 4:13

He giveth power to the faint; and to them that have no might he increaseth strength. Even the youths shall faint and be weary, and the young men shall utterly fall: But they that wait upon the LORD shall renew their strength; they shall mount up with wings as eagles; they shall run, and not be weary; and they shall walk, and not faint.

ISAIAH 40:29–31

Hear my cry, O God; attend unto my prayer. From the end of the earth will I cry unto thee, when my heart is overwhelmed: lead me to the rock that is higher than I. For thou hast been a shelter for me, and a strong tower from the enemy.

PSALM 61:1–3

Suffering

Take, my brethren, the prophets, who have spoken in the name of the Lord, for an example of suffering affliction, and of patience.

JAMES 5:10

It is a faithful saying: For if we be dead with him, we shall also live with him: If we suffer, we shall also reign with him: if we deny him, he also will deny us: If we believe not, yet he abideth faithful: he cannot deny himself.

2 TIMOTHY 2:11–13

Surely he hath borne our griefs, and carried our sorrows: yet we did esteem him stricken, smitten of God, and afflicted. But he was wounded for our transgressions, he was bruised for our iniquities: the chastisement of our peace was upon him; and with his stripes we are healed.

ISAIAH 53:4–5

For this is thankworthy, if a man for conscience toward God endure grief, suffering wrongfully. . . . For even hereunto were ye called: because Christ also suffered for us, leaving us an example, that ye should follow his steps: Who did no sin, neither was guile found in his mouth: Who, when he was reviled, reviled not again; when he suffered, he threatened not; but committed himself to him that judgeth righteously.

1 PETER 2:19, 21–23

For I reckon that the sufferings of this present time are not worthy to be compared with the glory which shall be revealed in us.

ROMANS 8:18

Beloved, think it not strange concerning the fiery trial which is to try you, as though some strange thing happened unto you: But rejoice, inasmuch as ye are partakers of Christ's sufferings; that, when his glory shall be revealed, ye may be glad also with exceeding joy.

1 PETER 4:12–13

And from the days of John the Baptist until now the kingdom of heaven suffereth violence, and the violent take it by force.

MATTHEW 11:12

For as the sufferings of Christ abound in us, so our consolation also aboundeth by Christ. And whether we be afflicted, it is for your consolation and salvation, which is effectual in the enduring of the same sufferings which we also suffer: or whether we be comforted, it is for your consolation and salvation.

2 CORINTHIANS 1:5–6

Yea, and all that will live godly in Christ Jesus shall suffer persecution.

2 TIMOTHY 3:12

But what things were gain to me, those I counted loss for Christ. Yea doubtless, and I count all things but loss for the excellency of the knowledge of Christ Jesus my Lord: for whom I have suffered the loss of all things, and do count them but dung, that I may win Christ, And be found in him. . .that I may know him, and the power of his resurrection, and the fellowship of his sufferings, being made conformable unto his death; If by any means I might attain unto the resurrection of the dead.

PHILIPPIANS 3:7–11

But we see Jesus, who was made a little lower than the angels for the suffering of death, crowned with glory and honour; that he by the grace of God should taste death for every man.

HEBREWS 2:9

Thankfulness

In every thing give thanks: for this is the will of God in Christ Jesus concerning you.

1 THESSALONIANS 5:18

And he took the seven loaves and the fishes, and gave thanks, and brake them, and gave to his disciples, and the disciples to the multitude.

MATTHEW 15:36

Giving thanks always for all things unto God and the Father in the name of our Lord Jesus Christ.

EPHESIANS 5:20

And they, continuing daily with one accord in the temple, and breaking bread from house to house, did eat their meat with gladness and singleness of heart, Praising God, and having favour with all the people. And the Lord added to the church daily such as should be saved.

ACTS 2:46–47

I will praise thee, O Lord, with my whole heart; I will shew forth all thy marvellous works. I will be glad and rejoice in thee: I will sing praise to thy name, O thou most High.

PSALM 9:1–2

Blessed be the Lord, that hath given rest unto his people Israel, according to all that he promised: there hath not failed one word of all his good promise, which he promised by the hand of Moses his servant.

1 KINGS 8:56

Blessed be the Lord, who daily loadeth us with benefits, even the God of our salvation. Selah.

PSALM 68:19

And he took the cup, and gave thanks, and gave it to them, saying, Drink ye all of it.

MATTHEW 26:27

O Lord, thou hast brought up my soul from the grave: thou hast kept me alive, that I should not go down to the pit.

Psalm 30:3

I will mention the lovingkindnesses of the Lord, and the praises of the Lord, according to all that the Lord hath bestowed on us, and the great goodness toward the house of Israel, which he hath bestowed on them according to his mercies, and according to the multitude of his lovingkindnesses.

Isaiah 63:7

Thou hast turned for me my mourning into dancing: thou hast put off my sackcloth, and girded me with gladness; To the end that my glory may sing praise to thee, and not be silent. O Lord my God, I will give thanks unto thee for ever.

Psalm 30:11–12

O give thanks unto the Lord; for he is good: for his mercy endureth for ever.

Psalm 136:1

That I may publish with the voice of thanksgiving, and tell of all thy wondrous works.

Psalm 26:7

I thank thee, and praise thee, O thou God of my fathers, who hast given me wisdom and might, and hast made known unto me now what we desired of thee: for thou hast now made known unto us the king's matter.

Daniel 2:23

And he took the cup, and gave thanks, and gave it to them, saying, Drink ye all of it.

Matthew 26:27

Many, O LORD my God, are thy wonderful works which thou hast done, and thy thoughts which are to us-ward: they cannot be reckoned up in order unto thee: if I would declare and speak of them, they are more than can be numbered.

PSALM 40:5

He that regardeth the day, regardeth it unto the Lord; and he that regardeth not the day, to the Lord he doth not regard it. He that eateth, eateth to the Lord, for he giveth God thanks; and he that eateth not, to the Lord he eateth not, and giveth God thanks.

ROMANS 14:6

It is a good thing to give thanks unto the LORD, and to sing praises unto thy name, O most High: To shew forth thy lovingkindness in the morning, and thy faithfulness every night.

PSALM 92:1–2

Trust

I will say of the Lord, He is my refuge and my fortress: my God; in him will I trust. . . . He shall cover thee with his feathers, and under his wings shalt thou trust: his truth shall be thy shield and buckler.

PSALM 91:2, 4

The Lord is my rock, and my fortress, and my deliverer; The God of my rock; in him will I trust: he is my shield, and the horn of my salvation, my high tower, and my refuge, my saviour; thou savest me from violence. I will call on the Lord, who is worthy to be praised: so shall I be saved from mine enemies.

2 SAMUEL 22:2–4

The Lord recompense thy work, and a full reward be given thee of the Lord God of Israel, under whose wings thou art come to trust.

RUTH 2:12

He shall not be afraid of evil tidings: his heart is fixed, trusting in the LORD.

PSALM 112:7

Behold my servant, whom I have chosen; my beloved, in whom my soul is well pleased: I will put my spirit upon him, and he shall shew judgment to the Gentiles. He shall not strive, nor cry; neither shall any man hear his voice in the streets. A bruised reed shall he not break, and smoking flax shall he not quench. . .And in his name shall the Gentiles trust.

MATTHEW 12:18–21

Trust in the LORD with all thine heart; and lean not unto thine own understanding. In all thy ways acknowledge him, and he shall direct thy paths.

PROVERBS 3:5–6

They that trust in the LORD shall be as mount Zion, which cannot be removed, but abideth for ever.

PSALM 125:1

222

Pray for us: for we trust we have a good conscience, in all things willing to live honestly.

HEBREWS 13:18

The LORD redeemeth the soul of his servants: and none of them that trust in him shall be desolate.

PSALM 34:22

For therefore we both labour and suffer reproach, because we trust in the living God, who is the Saviour of all men, specially of those that believe.

1 TIMOTHY 4:10

Be merciful unto me, O God, be merciful unto me: for my soul trusteth in thee: yea, in the shadow of thy wings will I make my refuge, until these calamities be overpast.

PSALM 57:1

It is better to trust in the LORD than to put confidence in man. It is better to trust in the LORD than to put confidence in princes.

PSALM 118:8–9

Truth

For the hope which is laid up for you in heaven, whereof ye heard before in the word of the truth of the gospel; Which is come unto you, as it is in all the world; and bringeth forth fruit, as it doth also in you, since the day ye heard of it, and knew the grace of God in truth.

COLOSSIANS 1:5–6

O send out thy light and thy truth: let them lead me; let them bring me unto thy holy hill, and to thy tabernacles.

PSALM 43:3

That we henceforth be no more children, tossed to and fro, and carried about with every wind of doctrine. . .But speaking the truth in love, may grow up into him in all things, which is the head, even Christ.

EPHESIANS 4:14–15

Master, we know that thou art true, and carest for no man: for thou regardest not the person of men, but teachest the way of God in truth.

MARK 12:14

Study to shew thyself approved unto God, a workman that needeth not to be ashamed, rightly dividing the word of truth.

2 TIMOTHY 2:15

For the wrath of God is revealed from heaven against all ungodliness and unrighteousness of men, who hold the truth in unrighteousness; Because that which may be known of God is manifest in them; for God hath shewed it unto them.

ROMANS 1:18–19

Lead me in thy truth, and teach me: for thou art the God of my salvation; on thee do I wait all the day.

PSALM 25:5

Sanctify them through thy truth: thy word is truth. As thou hast sent me into the world, even so have I also sent them into the world. And for their sakes I sanctify myself, that they also might be sanctified through the truth.

John 17:17–19

Behold, thou desirest truth in the inward parts: and in the hidden part thou shalt make me to know wisdom.

Psalm 51:6

And the Word was made flesh, and dwelt among us, (and we beheld his glory, the glory as of the only begotten of the Father,) full of grace and truth. . . . For the law was given by Moses, but grace and truth came by Jesus Christ.

John 1:14, 17

226

Understanding

❧❧❧ ❧❧❧

And of the children of Issachar, which were men that had understanding of the times, to know what Israel ought to do.

1 Chronicles 12:32

Take you wise men, and understanding, and known among your tribes, and I will make them rulers over you.

Deuteronomy 1:13

When wisdom entereth into thine heart, and knowledge is pleasant unto thy soul; Discretion shall preserve thee, understanding shall keep thee: To deliver thee from the way of the evil man, from the man that speaketh froward things; Who leave the paths of uprightness, to walk in the ways of darkness.

Proverbs 2:10–13

And all that heard him were astonished at his understanding and answers.

LUKE 2:47

And we know that the Son of God is come, and hath given us an understanding, that we may know him that is true, and we are in him that is true, even in his Son Jesus Christ.

1 JOHN 5:20

He that hath knowledge spareth his words: and a man of understanding is of an excellent spirit.

PROVERBS 17:27

Be ye not as the horse, or as the mule, which have no understanding: whose mouth must be held in with bit and bridle, lest they come near unto thee.

PSALM 32:9

And there shall come forth a rod out of the stem of Jesse, and a Branch shall grow out of his roots: And the spirit of the LORD shall rest upon him, the spirit of wisdom and understanding, the spirit of counsel and might, the spirit of knowledge and of the fear of the LORD; And shall make him of quick understanding in the fear of the LORD: and he shall not judge after the sight of his eyes, neither reprove after the hearing of his ears.

ISAIAH 11:1–3

Here is wisdom. Let him that hath understanding count the number of the beast: for it is the number of a man; and his number is Six hundred threescore and six.

REVELATION 13:18

What is it then? I will pray with the spirit, and I will pray with the understanding also: I will sing with the spirit, and I will sing with the understanding also.

1 CORINTHIANS 14:15

Who hath directed the spirit of the LORD, or being his counsellor hath taught him? With whom took he counsel, and who instructed him, and taught him in the path of judgment, and taught him knowledge, and shewed to him the way of understanding?

ISAIAH 40:13–14

As for these four children, God gave them knowledge and skill in all learning and wisdom: and Daniel had understanding in all visions and dreams.

DANIEL 1:17

Give me understanding, and I shall keep thy law; yea, I shall observe it with my whole heart. . . . Thy hands have made me and fashioned me: give me understanding, that I may learn thy commandments. . . . I am thy servant; give me understanding, that I may know thy testimonies.

PSALM 119:34, 73, 125

But where shall wisdom be found? and where is the place of understanding? Man knoweth not the price thereof; neither is it found in the land of the living. The depth saith, It is not in me: and the sea saith, It is not with me.

JOB 28:12–14

Let not mercy and truth forsake thee: bind them about thy neck; write them upon the table of thine heart: So shalt thou find favour and good understanding.

PROVERBS 3:3–4

The righteousness of thy testimonies is everlasting: give me understanding, and I shall live.

PSALM 119:144

Let my cry come near before thee, O LORD: give me understanding according to thy word.

PSALM 119:169

Wherefore I also. . .Cease not to give thanks for you, making mention of you in my prayers; That the God of our Lord Jesus Christ, the Father of glory, may give unto you the spirit of wisdom and revelation in the knowledge of him: The eyes of your understanding being enlightened; that ye may know what is the hope of his calling, and what the riches of the glory of his inheritance in the saints.

EPHESIANS 1:15–18

Great is our Lord, and of great power: his understanding is infinite.

PSALM 147:5

Through thy precepts I get understanding: therefore I hate every false way.

PSALM 119:104

The entrance of thy words giveth light; it giveth understanding unto the simple.

PSALM 119:130

Wisdom

And that from a child thou hast known the holy scriptures, which are able to make thee wise unto salvation through faith which is in Christ Jesus.

2 Timothy 3:15

Every wise woman buildeth her house: but the foolish plucketh it down with her hands.

Proverbs 14:1

Wisdom strengtheneth the wise more than ten mighty men which are in the city.

Ecclesiastes 7:19

See then that ye walk circumspectly, not as fools, but as wise, Redeeming the time, because the days are evil. Wherefore be ye not unwise, but understanding what the will of the Lord is.

Ephesians 5:15–17

But of him are ye in Christ Jesus, who of God is made unto us wisdom, and righteousness, and sanctification, and redemption: That, according as it is written, He that glorieth, let him glory in the Lord.

1 Corinthians 1:30–31

For we are labourers together with God: ye are God's husbandry, ye are God's building. According to the grace of God which is given unto me, as a wise masterbuilder, I have laid the foundation, and another buildeth thereon. But let every man take heed how he buildeth thereupon.

1 Corinthians 3:9–10

Be of the same mind one toward another. Mind not high things, but condescend to men of low estate. Be not wise in your own conceits.

Romans 12:16

The law of the LORD is perfect, converting the soul: the testimony of the LORD is sure, making wise the simple.

PSALM 19:7

In the mouth of the foolish is a rod of pride: but the lips of the wise shall preserve them.

PROVERBS 14:3

Now unto the King eternal, immortal, invisible, the only wise God, be honour and glory for ever and ever. Amen.

1 TIMOTHY 1:17

But the wisdom that is from above is first pure, then peaceable, gentle, and easy to be intreated, full of mercy and good fruits, without partiality, and without hypocrisy.

JAMES 3:17

If any of you lack wisdom, let him ask of God, that giveth to all men liberally, and upbraideth not; and it shall be given him. But let him ask in faith, nothing wavering. For he that wavereth is like a wave of the sea driven with the wind and tossed. For let not that man think that he shall receive any thing of the Lord. A double minded man is unstable in all his ways.

JAMES 1:5–8

And they that be wise shall shine as the brightness of the firmament; and they that turn many to righteousness as the stars for ever and ever.

DANIEL 12:3

The wise in heart shall be called prudent: and the sweetness of the lips increaseth learning. . . . The heart of the wise teacheth his mouth, and addeth learning to his lips.

PROVERBS 16:21, 23

Worship

The four and twenty elders fall down before him that sat on the throne, and worship him that liveth for ever and ever, and cast their crowns before the throne, saying, Thou art worthy, O Lord, to receive glory and honour and power: for thou hast created all things, and for thy pleasure they are and were created.

REVELATION 4:10–11

God is a Spirit: and they that worship him must worship him in spirit and in truth.

JOHN 4:24

For thou shalt worship no other god: for the LORD, whose name is Jealous, is a jealous God.

EXODUS 34:14

Give unto the LORD the glory due unto his name: bring an offering, and come before him: worship the LORD in the beauty of holiness.

1 CHRONICLES 16:29

Then saith Jesus unto him, Get thee hence, Satan: for it is written, Thou shalt worship the Lord thy God, and him only shalt thou serve.

MATTHEW 4:10

And I fell at his feet to worship him. And he said unto me, See thou do it not: I am thy fellowservant, and of thy brethren that have the testimony of Jesus: worship God: for the testimony of Jesus is the spirit of prophecy.

REVELATION 19:10

But the hour cometh, and now is, when the true worshippers shall worship the Father in spirit and in truth: for the Father seeketh such to worship him.

JOHN 4:23

Who shall not fear thee, O Lord, and glorify thy name? for thou only art holy: for all nations shall come and worship before thee; for thy judgments are made manifest.

REVELATION 15:4

Encouragement Just for Moms!

Encouraging Words for Mothers: Morning & Evening

This 365-day morning and evening devotional book is written *by* a mom—award-winning writer Michelle Medlock Adams—*for* moms. Especially for women with children still at home, it offers brief, relevant, and biblical reflections with monthly themes such as worry, unconditional love, discipline, and praying, showing how scripture applies to your everyday life.

Flexible Casebound / 978-1-64352-080-3 / $19.99

Bible Prayers for Mothers

Featuring easy-to-read devotions, relevant scriptures, and a practical application section, *Bible Prayers for Mothers* offers encouraging, even life-changing blessings for your quiet time.

Paperback / 978-1-64352-309-5 / $5.99